HOLIDAY
ENTERTAINING

Publications International, Ltd.

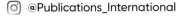

Let's get social!
🔲 @Publications_International
🔲 @PublicationsInternational
www.pilbooks.com

APPETIZERS
& SNACKS

CONTENTS

STUFFED MUSHROOM CAPS
Makes 24 mushrooms

2 packages (8 ounces each) whole mushrooms (24 mushrooms)

1 tablespoon butter

⅔ cup finely chopped cooked chicken or coarsely chopped pecans or walnuts

1 tablespoon chopped fresh basil

2 teaspoons lemon juice

¼ teaspoon onion powder

⅛ teaspoon salt

⅛ teaspoon garlic powder

⅛ teaspoon black pepper

¼ cup grated Parmesan cheese

3 ounces cream cheese, softened

Paprika

1. Preheat oven to 350°F. Remove stems from mushrooms and finely chop. Arrange mushroom caps top sides down on greased baking sheet.

2. Melt butter in medium skillet over medium-high heat. Add chopped mushrooms; cook and stir 5 minutes. Add chicken, basil, lemon juice, onion powder, salt, garlic powder and pepper; cook and stir 5 minutes. Remove from heat; stir in Parmesan cheese and cream cheese. Spoon mixture evenly into mushroom caps.

3. Bake 10 to 15 minutes or until heated through. Sprinkle with paprika.

Cocktail Party Menu

Strawberry Champagne Punch, page 178

Sparkling Pomegranate Gingerade, page 184

Apricot and Brie Dip, page 48

Celebration Cheeseball, page 34

Barbecued Meatballs, page 10

Balsamic Onion and Prosciutto Pizzettes, page 20

Quattro Formaggio Focaccia, page 136

Chocolate Caramel Thumbprint Cookies, page 156

Little Christmas Truffles, page 162

MOZZARELLA AND PROSCIUTTO BITES
Makes 16 pieces

16 small bamboo skewers or toothpicks

8 ounces fresh mozzarella

¼ cup chopped fresh basil

½ teaspoon black pepper

6 thin slices prosciutto

• •

1. Soak skewers in water 20 minutes to prevent burning. Cut mozzarella into 16 chunks (about 1-inch pieces).* Place on paper towel-lined plate; sprinkle with basil and pepper, turning to coat all sides.

2. Cut prosciutto slices crosswise into thirds. Tightly wrap one prosciutto slice around each piece of mozzarella, covering completely. Insert skewer into each piece; place on cutting board or baking sheet. Freeze 15 minutes to firm.

3. Preheat broiler. Line broiler pan or baking sheet with foil. Place skewers on prepared pan; broil about 3 minutes or until prosciutto begins to crisp, turning once. Serve immediately.

You can also substitute one 8-ounce container of small fresh mozzarella balls (ciliengini). One 8-ounce container contains 24 balls.

BARBECUED MEATBALLS
Makes about 4 dozen meatballs

2 pounds ground beef

1⅓ cups ketchup, divided

1 egg, lightly beaten

3 tablespoons seasoned dry bread crumbs

2 tablespoons dried onion flakes

¾ teaspoon garlic salt

½ teaspoon black pepper

1 cup packed brown sugar

1 can (6 ounces) tomato paste

¼ cup reduced-sodium soy sauce

¼ cup cider vinegar

1½ teaspoons hot pepper sauce

• •

Slow Cooker Directions

1. Preheat oven to 350°F. Combine beef, ⅓ cup ketchup, egg, bread crumbs, onion flakes, garlic salt and black pepper in large bowl. Mix lightly but thoroughly; shape into 1-inch meatballs.

2. Arrange meatballs in single layer on two 15×10-inch baking pans. Bake 18 minutes or until browned. Transfer meatballs to slow cooker.

3. Combine remaining 1 cup ketchup, brown sugar, tomato paste, soy sauce, vinegar and hot pepper sauce in medium bowl. Pour over meatballs. Cover; cook on LOW 4 hours.

Barbecued Franks

Arrange two (12-ounce) packages or three (8-ounce) packages cocktail franks in slow cooker. Prepare ketchup mixture as directed in step 3; pour over franks. Cover; cook on LOW 4 hours.

MINI SPINACH AND BACON QUICHES
Makes 12 servings

3 slices bacon

½ small onion, diced

1 package (10 ounces) frozen chopped spinach, thawed and squeezed dry

½ teaspoon black pepper

⅛ teaspoon ground nutmeg

Pinch of salt

3 eggs

1 container (15 ounces) whole-milk ricotta cheese

2 cups (8 ounces) shredded mozzarella cheese

1 cup grated Parmesan cheese

• •

1. Preheat oven to 350°F. Spray 12 standard (2½-inch) muffin cups with nonstick cooking spray.

2. Cook bacon in large skillet over medium-high heat until crisp. Drain on paper towel lined-plate. Crumble bacon when until cool enough to handle.

3. Heat same skillet with bacon drippings over medium heat. Add onion; cook and stir 5 minutes or until softened. Add spinach, pepper, nutmeg and salt; cook and stir 3 minutes or until liquid is evaporated. Remove from heat. Stir in bacon; set aside to cool.

4. Whisk eggs in large bowl. Add cheeses; stir until well blended. Add spinach mixture; mix well. Spoon evenly into prepared muffin cups.

5. Bake 40 minutes or until set. Cool in pan 10 minutes. Run thin knife around edges to remove from pan. Serve warm or at room temperature.

CITRUS CANDIED NUTS →
Makes about 3 cups

1 egg white
¼ teaspoon salt
1½ cups whole almonds
1½ cups pecan halves
1 cup powdered sugar

2 tablespoons lemon juice
2 teaspoons grated orange peel
1 teaspoon grated lemon peel
⅛ teaspoon ground nutmeg

• •

1. Preheat oven to 300°F. Lightly grease large baking sheet.

2. Beat egg white and salt in medium bowl with electric mixer at high speed until soft peaks form. Add almonds and pecans; stir until well coated. Stir in powdered sugar, lemon juice, orange peel, lemon peel and nutmeg until evenly coated. Spread nuts in single layer on prepared pan.

3. Bake 30 minutes, stirring after 20 minutes. Turn off heat. Let nuts stand in oven 15 minutes. Spread nuts on large sheet of foil; cool completely.

ROSEMARY NUT MIX
Makes about 2 cups

2 tablespoons butter
2 cups pecan halves
1 cup unsalted macadamia nuts
1 cup walnuts

1 teaspoon dried rosemary
½ teaspoon salt
¼ teaspoon red pepper flakes

• •

1. Preheat oven to 300°F.

2. Melt butter in large saucepan over low heat. Stir in pecans, macadamia nuts and walnuts. Add rosemary, salt and red pepper flakes; cook and stir about 1 minute. Spread mixture on ungreased baking sheet.

3. Bake 8 to 10 minutes or until nuts are fragrant and lightly browned, stirring once. Cool completely on baking sheet on wire rack.

CLASSIC DEVILED EGGS
Makes 12 deviled eggs

6 eggs

3 tablespoons mayonnaise

½ teaspoon apple cider vinegar

½ teaspoon yellow mustard

⅛ teaspoon salt

Optional toppings: black pepper, paprika, minced fresh chives and/or minced red onion (optional)

• •

1. Bring medium saucepan of water to a boil. Gently add eggs with slotted spoon. Reduce heat to maintain a simmer; cook 12 minutes. Meanwhile, fill medium bowl with cold water and ice cubes. Drain eggs and place in ice water; cool 10 minutes.

2. Carefully peel eggs. Cut eggs in half; place yolks in small bowl. Add mayonnaise, vinegar, mustard and salt; mash until well blended. Spoon mixture into egg whites; garnish with desired toppings.

Tip
For a fancier presentation, pipe filling into egg whites using a pastry bag and a large star tip.

GOAT CHEESE CROSTINI WITH SWEET ONION JAM
Makes 24 crostini

1 tablespoon olive oil

2 medium yellow onions, thinly sliced

¾ cup dry red wine

¼ cup water

2 tablespoons packed brown sugar

1 tablespoon balsamic vinegar

1 teaspoon salt

¼ teaspoon black pepper

2 ounces soft goat cheese

2 ounces cream cheese, softened

1 teaspoon chopped fresh thyme, plus additional for garnish

1 loaf (16 ounces) French bread, cut into 24 slices (about 1 inch thick), lightly toasted

• •

1. Heat oil in large skillet over medium heat. Add onions; cook and stir 10 minutes. Add wine, water, brown sugar, vinegar, salt and pepper; bring to a simmer. Reduce heat to low. Cook, uncovered, 15 to 20 minutes or until all liquid is absorbed. (If mixture appears dry, stir in a few tablespoons of additional water.) Cool 30 minutes or cover and refrigerate until ready to use.

2. Meanwhile, mix goat cheese, cream cheese and 1 teaspoon thyme in small bowl until well blended. Spread ½ teaspoon goat cheese mixture on each slice of toast. Top with 1 teaspoon onion jam. Garnish with additional thyme.

BALSAMIC ONION AND PROSCIUTTO PIZZETTES
Makes 16 pizzettes

1 package (16 ounces) refrigerated pizza dough*

2 tablespoons olive oil, divided

1 large or 2 small red onions, halved and thinly sliced

¼ teaspoon salt

1½ tablespoons balsamic vinegar

⅛ teaspoon black pepper

⅔ cup grated Parmesan cheese

4 ounces fresh mozzarella, cut into small pieces

1 package (about 3 ounces) thinly sliced prosciutto, cut or torn into small pieces

Frozen pizza dough can also be used. Thaw according to package directions.

• •

1. Remove dough from refrigerator; let rest at room temperature while preparing onions. Heat 1 tablespoon oil in medium skillet over medium-high heat. Add onion and salt; cook about 20 minutes or until tender and golden brown, stirring occasionally. Add vinegar and pepper; cook and stir 2 minutes. Set aside to cool.

2. Preheat oven to 450°F. Line two baking sheets with parchment paper.

3. Divide dough into 16 balls; press into 3-inch rounds (about ⅜ inch thick) on prepared baking sheets. Brush rounds with remaining 1 tablespoon oil; sprinkle each with about 1 teaspoon Parmesan. Top with onions, mozzarella, prosciutto and remaining Parmesan.

4. Bake about 13 minutes or until crusts are golden brown.

LEEK STRUDELS
Makes 9 servings

1 tablespoon butter

1 tablespoon olive oil

2 pounds leeks, cleaned and
  sliced (white parts only)

¼ teaspoon caraway seeds

¼ teaspoon salt

⅛ teaspoon white pepper

¼ cup dry white wine or water

3 sheets frozen phyllo dough,
  thawed

Butter-flavored nonstick
  cooking spray

• •

1. Heat butter and oil in large skillet over medium heat. Add leeks; cook and stir about 5 minutes or until tender. Stir in caraway seeds, salt and pepper. Add wine; bring to a boil over high heat. Reduce heat to low. Simmer, covered, about 5 minutes or until wine is absorbed. Let mixture cool to room temperature.

2. Preheat oven to 400°F. Cut each sheet of phyllo dough lengthwise into thirds. Spray one piece of dough with nonstick cooking spray; spoon 2 tablespoons leek mixture near bottom of piece. Fold one corner over filling to make triangle. Continue folding, as you would fold a flag, to make triangular packet.

3. Repeat with remaining phyllo dough and leek mixture. Place packets on ungreased baking sheet; lightly coat tops of packets with cooking spray. Bake about 20 minutes or until golden brown. Serve warm.

CHIPOTLE-HONEY CHICKEN MEATBALLS
Makes 48 meatballs

2 pounds ground chicken

2 eggs, lightly beaten

⅓ cup plain dry bread crumbs

⅓ cup chopped fresh cilantro

3 tablespoons lime juice, divided

4 cloves garlic, minced

1 can (4 ounces) chipotle peppers in adobo sauce, divided

1½ teaspoon salt, divided

¾ cup honey

⅓ cup chicken broth

⅓ cup tomato paste

2 teaspoons Dijon mustard

2 tablespoons vegetable oil

• •

1. Line two baking sheets with parchment paper. Combine chicken, eggs, bread crumbs, cilantro, 2 tablespoons lime juice, garlic, 1 tablespoon adobo sauce and 1 teaspoon salt in medium bowl; mix well. Shape mixture into 48 meatballs. Place meatballs on prepared baking sheets. Cover with plastic wrap; refrigerate 1 hour.

2. Combine 2 chipotle peppers, honey, broth, tomato paste, 1 tablespoon lime juice, mustard and remaining ½ teaspoon salt in food processor or blender; process until smooth.

3. Preheat oven to 400°F. Brush meatballs with oil. Bake 12 minutes. Transfer meatballs to large baking dish. Add sauce; stir until coated. Bake 10 minutes or until meatballs are heated through and glazed with sauce.

FESTIVE CRAB TOASTS
Makes about 30 appetizers

12 ounces crabmeat, flaked

1 can (10¾ ounces) condensed cream of celery soup, undiluted

¼ cup chopped celery

¼ cup sliced green onions

1 tablespoon lemon juice

⅛ teaspoon grated lemon peel

1 (8-ounce) French bread baguette

⅓ cup grated Parmesan cheese

Paprika

• •

1. Combine crabmeat, soup, celery, green onions, lemon juice and lemon peel in medium bowl; mix well. Cut baguette diagonally into ½-inch slices; arrange slices on two ungreased baking sheets. Broil 5 inches from heat 2 minutes or until toasted, turning once.

2. Spread 1 tablespoon crab mixture onto each baguette slice. Sprinkle with Parmesan cheese and paprika. Broil 5 inches from heat 2 minutes or until lightly browned.

DIPS & CHEESEBALLS

SPINACH-ARTICHOKE DIP
Makes 6 to 8 servings

1 package (8 ounces) baby spinach*

1 package (8 ounces) cream cheese, softened

¼ cup mayonnaise

1 clove garlic, minced

1 teaspoon dried basil

½ teaspoon dried thyme

¼ teaspoon salt

¼ teaspoon red pepper flakes

¼ teaspoon black pepper

1 can (about 14 ounces) artichoke hearts, drained and chopped

¾ cup grated Parmesan cheese, divided

Toasted French bread slices, pita chips or tortilla chips

Or substitute 1 package (10 ounces) frozen chopped spinach, thawed and squeezed dry. Proceed with step 3.

• •

1. Preheat oven to 350°F. Spray 8-inch oval, round or square baking dish with nonstick cooking spray.

2. Place spinach in large microwavable bowl; cover and microwave on HIGH 2 minutes or until wilted. Uncover; let stand until cool enough to handle. Squeeze dry and coarsely chop.

3. Whisk cream cheese, mayonnaise, garlic, basil, thyme, salt, red pepper flakes and black pepper in medium bowl until well blended. Stir in spinach, artichokes and ½ cup Parmesan. Spread in prepared baking dish; sprinkle with remaining ¼ cup Parmesan.

4. Bake about 30 minutes or until edges are golden brown. Cool slightly; serve warm with toasted bread slices.

TIROKAFTERI (SPICY GREEK FETA SPREAD)
Makes 2 cups

2 small hot red peppers

½ small clove garlic

1 block (8 ounces) feta cheese

¾ cup plain Greek yogurt

1 tablespoon lemon juice

½ teaspoon salt

Toasted French bread slices and/or cut-up fresh vegetables

1. Preheat oven to 400°F. Place peppers on small piece of foil on baking sheet. Bake 15 minutes or until peppers are soft and charred. Cool completely. Scrape off skin with paring knife. Cut off top and remove seeds. Place peppers in food processor. Add garlic; pulse until finely chopped.

2. Add feta, yogurt, lemon juice and salt; pulse until well blended but still chunky. Serve with bread and vegetables. Store leftovers in airtight container in refrigerator up to 2 weeks.

Holiday Appetizer Board

Tirokafteri (Spicy Greek Feta Spread)

Garlic and Herb Dip, page 46

Rosemary Nut Mix, page 14

Cheddar Quick Bread (cut into cubes for dipping), page 130

Carrot sticks, celery sticks, bell pepper strips or halved mini peppers, grape tomatoes, pita chips and pitted Kalamata olives

CELEBRATION CHEESEBALL
Makes about 2½ cups

2 packages (8 ounces each) cream cheese, softened

⅓ cup mayonnaise

¼ cup grated Parmesan cheese

2 tablespoons finely chopped carrot

1 tablespoon finely chopped red onion

1½ teaspoons prepared horseradish

¼ teaspoon salt

½ cup chopped pecans or walnuts

Assorted crackers

• •

1. Combine cream cheese, mayonnaise, Parmesan, carrot, onion, horseradish and salt in medium bowl until well blended. Cover and refrigerate until firm.

2. Shape cheese mixture into a ball with dampened hands; roll in pecans. Wrap cheese ball in plastic wrap and refrigerate at least 1 hour. Serve with assorted crackers.

ONION AND WHITE BEAN SPREAD
Makes 1¼ cups spread

1 can (about 15 ounces) cannellini or Great Northern beans, rinsed and drained

¼ cup chopped green onions

¼ cup grated Parmesan cheese

¼ cup olive oil, plus additional for serving

1 tablespoon fresh rosemary, chopped

2 cloves garlic, minced

Salt and black pepper

Toasted French bread slices

• •

1. Combine beans, green onions, Parmesan, ¼ cup oil, rosemary and garlic in food processor; process 30 to 40 seconds or until almost smooth. Season to taste with salt and pepper.

2. Spoon bean mixture into serving bowl. Drizzle additional oil over spread just before serving. Serve with toasted bread slices.

Tip

For a more rustic looking spread,
place all ingredients in a medium bowl
and mash them with a potato masher.

THREE-CHEESE PECAN BALL
Makes 2 cheese balls

1 can (8 ounces) crushed pineapple in heavy syrup, drained

2 cups toasted* pecan pieces, divided

1 package (8 ounces) cream cheese, softened

2 cups (8 ounces) finely shredded sharp Cheddar cheese

¾ cup crumbled blue cheese

2 tablespoons Worcestershire sauce

1 teaspoon sugar

½ teaspoon red pepper flakes

Assorted crackers or pretzel twists

To toast pecans, cook in medium skillet over medium heat 3 to 4 minutes or until lightly browned and fragrant, stirring frequently.

1. Combine drained pineapple, 1 cup pecans, cream cheese, Cheddar cheese, blue cheese, Worcestershire sauce, sugar and red pepper flakes in large bowl.

2. Shape mixture into two balls or rolls; roll in remaining pecans to coat. Cover with plastic wrap. Freeze 30 minutes or refrigerate 2 hours or until firm. Serve with crackers.

CHEESY FONDUE
Makes 6 to 8 servings

2 cups (8 ounces) shredded Swiss cheese

2 cups (8 ounces) shredded Monterey Jack cheese

2 tablespoons all-purpose flour

1½ cups dry white wine or apple juice

Dash ground nutmeg

Dash ground red pepper

1 French bread loaf, cut into cubes

Sliced Granny Smith apples and/or pears

• •

1. Combine cheeses and flour in large bowl; toss lightly to coat.

2. Bring wine to a simmer over medium heat in fondue pot. Gradually add cheese mixture until melted, stirring constantly. Stir in nutmeg and pepper. Keep warm in fondue pot or small slow cooker, stirring occasionally. Serve with bread cubes and apple for dipping.

STEWED FIG AND BLUE CHEESE DIP
Makes 6 to 8 servings

1 tablespoon olive oil

1 onion, chopped

½ cup port wine

1 package (6 ounces) dried figs,
   finely chopped

½ cup orange juice

½ cup crumbled blue cheese,
   divided

1 tablespoon butter

Assorted crackers

• •

Slow Cooker Directions

1. Heat oil in small nonstick skillet over medium-high heat. Add onion; cook 7 minutes or until light golden, stirring occasionally. Stir in port and bring to a boil; cook 1 minute. Transfer to 1½-quart slow cooker; stir in figs and orange juice.

2. Cover; cook on HIGH 1 to 1½ hours or until figs are plump and tender. Stir in ¼ cup blue cheese and butter. Transfer to serving bowl. Sprinkle with remaining blue cheese. Serve with assorted crackers.

BAKED BRIE WITH NUT CRUST
Makes 8 servings

⅓ cup pecans

⅓ cup almonds

⅓ cup walnuts

1 egg

1 tablespoon whipping cream

1 round (8 ounces) Brie cheese

2 tablespoons raspberry jam

Assorted crackers

1. Preheat oven to 350°F. Pulse nuts in food processor until finely chopped. *Do not over process.* Place nuts in shallow bowl.

2. Combine egg and cream in another shallow dish; whisk until well blended.

3. Dip Brie into egg mixture, then into nut mixture, turning to coat. Press nuts to adhere.

4. Place Brie on small baking sheet; spread jam over top. Bake 15 minutes or until cheese is warm and soft. Serve with crackers for dipping.

Tip

For a spectacular snack spread, present various contrasting options. Serve a warm, soft spread like this one with something crunchy (Citrus Candied Nuts, page 14), something zesty (Chipotle-Honey Chicken Meatballs, page 24) and something light and fresh (Lemony Ranch Dip, page 48).

GARLIC AND HERB DIP →
Makes about 1¼ cups

1 cup sour cream

¼ cup mayonnaise

2 tablespoons chopped green onion

1 teaspoon dried basil

½ teaspoon dried tarragon

1 clove garlic, minced

¼ teaspoon salt

¼ teaspoon black pepper

Cut-up fresh vegetables and/or pita chips

· ·

Whisk sour cream, mayonnaise, green onions, basil, tarragon, garlic, salt and pepper. Cover and refrigerate several hours or overnight. Serve with vegetables.

EASY FRIED ONION DIP
Makes about 2 cups

1 container (16 ounces) sour cream

3 tablespoons Worcestershire sauce

1 can (about 3 ounces) French fried onions

Ruffle potato chips and/or pretzel sticks or twists

· ·

Combine sour cream and Worcestershire sauce in medium bowl until well blended. Stir in French fried onions just until combined. Serve with potato chips.

APRICOT AND BRIE DIP →
Makes 3 cups

½ cup dried apricots, finely chopped

⅓ cup plus 1 tablespoon apricot preserves, divided

¼ cup apple juice

2 pounds Brie cheese, rind removed and cut into cubes

Assorted crackers

• •

Slow Cooker Directions

1. Combine dried apricots, ⅓ cup apricot preserves and apple juice in slow cooker. Cover; cook on HIGH 40 minutes.

2. Stir in cheese. Cover; cook on HIGH 30 minutes or until melted. Stir in remaining 1 tablespoon preserves. Serve with crackers.

LEMONY RANCH DIP
Makes 2 cups

¾ cup mayonnaise

½ cup buttermilk

¼ cup sour cream

2 tablespoons grated lemon peel

1 tablespoon fresh lemon juice

1 clove garlic, minced

1 tablespoon fresh chives

1 tablespoon fresh basil

1 tablespoon fresh dill

½ teaspoon salt

Cut-up fresh vegetables

• •

Combine mayonnaise, buttermilk, sour cream, lemon peel, lemon juice, garlic, chives, basil, dill and salt in food processor or blender; process until combined. Serve with vegetables.

THREE-CHEESE ROASTED GARLIC SPREAD
Makes 2½ cups

2 heads garlic

1 tablespoon olive oil

2 packages (8 ounces each) cream cheese, softened

1 package (3½ ounces) goat cheese

2 tablespoons crumbled blue cheese, plus additional for garnish

1 teaspoon dried thyme

Fresh thyme (optional)

Cut-up vegetables and/or kettle-cooked potato chips

• •

1. Preheat oven to 400°F. Cut tops of garlic just to expose tops of cloves. Place garlic on 10-inch piece of foil; drizzle with oil and crimp shut. Place on small baking sheet; bake 30 minutes or until tender. Cool 15 minutes; squeeze cloves into small bowl. Mash into smooth paste.

2. Beat cream cheese and goat cheese in medium bowl until smooth. Stir in garlic, 2 tablespoons blue cheese and dried thyme. Cover and refrigerate 3 hours or overnight.

3. Spoon dip into serving bowl. Garnish with additional blue cheese and fresh thyme. Serve with vegetables.

CENTERPIECE MEATS

BAKED HAM WITH SWEET AND SPICY GLAZE
Makes 8 to 10 servings

1 bone-in smoked half ham
(8 pounds)

¾ cup packed brown sugar

⅓ cup cider vinegar

¼ cup golden raisins

1 can (8¾ ounces) sliced peaches
in heavy syrup, drained,
chopped and syrup reserved

1 tablespoon cornstarch

¼ cup orange juice

1 can (8¼ ounces) crushed
pineapple in syrup,
undrained

1 tablespoon grated orange peel

1 clove garlic, minced

½ teaspoon red pepper flakes

½ teaspoon grated fresh ginger

• •

1. Preheat oven to 325°F. Place ham, fat side up, in roasting pan. Bake 3 hours.

2. Meanwhile for glaze, combine brown sugar, vinegar, raisins and peach syrup in medium saucepan. Bring to a boil over high heat. Reduce heat to low; simmer 8 to 10 minutes.

3. Whisk cornstarch into orange juice in small bowl until smooth and well blended. Stir into brown sugar mixture. Stir peaches, pineapple, orange peel, garlic, red pepper flakes and ginger into saucepan; bring to a boil over medium heat. Cook until sauce is thickened, stirring constantly.

4. Remove ham from oven. Generously brush half of glaze over ham; bake 30 minutes or until thermometer inserted into thickest part of ham registers 160°F.

5. Remove ham from oven; pour remaining glaze over ham. Let stand 20 minutes before slicing.

SIMPLE ROASTED CHICKEN
Makes 4 servings

1 whole chicken (4 to 5 pounds)

3 tablespoons butter, softened

1½ teaspoons salt

1 teaspoon onion powder

1 teaspoon dried thyme

½ teaspoon garlic powder

½ teaspoon paprika

½ teaspoon black pepper

• •

1. Preheat oven to 425°F. Pat chicken dry; place in small baking dish or on baking sheet.

2. Combine butter, salt, onion powder, thyme, garlic powder, paprika and pepper in small microwavable bowl; mash with fork until well blended. Loosen skin on breasts and thighs; spread about one third of butter mixture under skin.

3. Microwave remaining butter mixture until melted. Brush melted butter mixture all over outside of chicken and inside cavity. Tie drumsticks together with kitchen string and tuck wing tips under.

4. Roast 20 minutes. *Reduce oven temperature to 375°F.* Roast 45 to 55 minutes or until chicken is cooked through (165°F), basting once with pan juices during last 10 minutes of cooking time. Remove chicken to large cutting board; tent with foil. Let stand 15 minutes before carving.

TUSCAN PORK LOIN ROAST WITH FIG SAUCE
Makes 6 to 8 servings

2 tablespoons olive oil

3 cloves garlic, minced

2 teaspoons coarse salt

2 teaspoons dried rosemary

½ teaspoon red pepper flakes *or* 1 teaspoon black pepper

1 center cut boneless pork loin roast (about 3 pounds)

¼ cup dry red wine

1 jar (about 8 ounces) fig jam

• •

1. Preheat oven to 350°F. Combine oil, garlic, salt, rosemary and red pepper flakes in small bowl; brush over roast. Place pork on rack in shallow roasting pan.

2. Roast 1 hour or until internal temperature registers 160°F on instant-read thermometer. Transfer to cutting board. Tent with foil; let stand 10 minutes.

3. Meanwhile, pour wine into roasting pan. Place pan on one or two burners on stovetop; cook over medium-high heat 2 minutes, stirring to scrape up browned bits. Stir in fig jam; cook and stir until heated through. Slice pork; serve with sauce.

Italian-Inspired Menu

Kir, page 176

Mozzarella and Prosciutto Bites, page 8

Onion and White Bean Spread, page 36

Tuscan Pork Loin Roast with Fig Sauce

Green Beans Gremolata, page 106

Parmesan Alfredo Pasta Bake, page 104

Pesto Rolls, page 132

Fruitcake Cookies, page 144

TURKEY WITH APPLE CORN BREAD STUFFING
Makes 14 servings

STUFFING

1 package (12 ounces) bacon, cut into ½-inch pieces

4 cups chopped onions

3 cups chopped celery

6 cups chopped peeled apples

1 package (12 ounces) corn bread stuffing mix

1 cup chopped pecans, toasted

1½ teaspoons dried thyme

1 teaspoon dried sage

2½ cups chicken broth

½ cup (1 stick) butter

Salt and black pepper

TURKEY

1 cup apple jelly

1 cup apple juice

¼ cup white balsamic vinegar

¼ cup honey

½ teaspoon salt

1 whole turkey (16 to 18 pounds), thawed if frozen

2 tablespoons vegetable or olive oil

GRAVY

¼ cup all-purpose flour

2 cans (about 14 ounces each) chicken broth

• •

1. For stuffing, cook bacon in large skillet over medium heat until crisp, stirring occasionally. Remove bacon with slotted spoon; drain on paper towel-lined plate. Drain drippings, reserving 2 tablespoons in skillet. Heat same skillet over medium-high heat. Add onion and celery; cook and stir 15 to 20 minutes or until very tender. Transfer vegetable mixture to large bowl; stir in bacon, apples, stuffing mix, pecans, thyme and sage. Stir in broth and butter. Season to taste with salt and black pepper. Reserve 7 cups stuffing mixture for turkey; spread remaining stuffing in 1½-quart baking dish. Cover baking dish and set aside until turkey has finished cooking.

2. Preheat oven to 325°F. For glaze, combine jelly, juice, vinegar, honey and ½ teaspoon salt in small saucepan. Bring to a boil over medium-high heat. Reduce heat to low; simmer about 15 minutes or until reduced to 1¼ cups, stirring occasionally. Reserve ¼ cup mixture for gravy.

3. For turkey, remove neck and giblets from turkey; discard or reserve for another use. Place turkey on rack in large roasting pan, breast side up. Pat turkey dry with paper towels. Fill neck cavity with some of stuffing. Turn

wings back to hold neck skin against back of turkey. Fill body cavity with remaining stuffing. Brush turkey all over with oil. Cover skin of neck cavity and stuffing at body cavity opening with foil. Brush some of glaze all over turkey. Roast 2 hours (cover turkey with foil if browning too quickly).

4. Brush turkey with additional glaze. Roast until instant-read thermometer inserted into thickest part of thigh not touching bone registers 165°F. Remove turkey from oven and place reserved baking dish of stuffing in oven; bake 45 minutes, removing cover for last 15 minutes. Let turkey stand at least 20 minutes. Remove stuffing and carve turkey.

5. For gravy, pour pan drippings into 1-quart liquid measuring cup; skim fat. Pour drippings into medium saucepan; whisk in flour until smooth. Add reserved ¼ cup glaze and enough broth to make 3½ cups. Bring to a boil over medium-high heat. Reduce heat to low; simmer 3 to 5 minutes or until thickened, stirring frequently.

BEEF RIB ROAST WITH MUSHROOM-BACON SAUCE
Makes 4 to 6 servings

ROAST

4 to 5 cloves garlic

1 tablespoon kosher salt

1 tablespoon chopped fresh thyme

1 tablespoon chopped fresh basil

1 tablespoon black pepper

3 tablespoons olive oil

1 beef rib roast (6 to 8 pounds), trimmed

MUSHROOM-BACON SAUCE

4 slices bacon, chopped

1 shallot, diced

1 pound sliced mushrooms

6 cups beef broth

1 cup dry red wine

2 tablespoons butter

Salt and black pepper

. . . .

1. Place garlic, salt, thyme, basil and pepper in food processor. Process until garlic is finely chopped. Add oil in slow stream, processing until paste forms.

2. Pat roast dry; place bone side down on rack in shallow roasting pan. Cut several small slits in fat layer across top of roast. Rub garlic paste over entire roast. Cover; refrigerate at least 4 hours or up to 1 day.

3. Preheat oven to 450°F. Bake roast 20 minutes. *Reduce oven temperature to 350°F.* Bake 1 hour 30 minutes or until instant-read thermometer inserted into center registers 140°F for medium-rare or 150°F for medium. Remove roast to cutting board; cover and let stand 20 minutes before slicing.

4. Meanwhile for sauce, cook bacon in medium saucepan over medium heat until lightly browned. Add shallot; cook and stir 2 minutes. Add mushrooms; cook and stir 8 minutes or until bacon is crisp. Set aside.

5. Bring broth and wine to a boil in large saucepan over medium-high heat. Reduce heat to low; simmer 20 minutes or until mixture is reduced to about 2 cups. (This can be done up to 2 days ahead. Cover both mushroom mixture and broth mixture separately and refrigerate.)

6. Place roasting pan on one or two burners on stovetop. Add mushroom mixture and broth mixture; cook and stir over medium heat 5 minutes or until sauce is slightly thickened. Whisk in butter; season with salt and pepper. Serve with roast.

APPLE STUFFED PORK LOIN ROAST
Makes 14 to 16 servings

2 cloves garlic, minced

1 teaspoon coarse salt

1 teaspoon dried rosemary

½ teaspoon dried thyme

½ teaspoon black pepper

1 boneless center cut pork loin roast (4 to 5 pounds)

1 tablespoon butter

2 large tart apples, peeled and thinly sliced (about 2 cups)

1 medium onion, cut into thin strips (about 1 cup)

2 tablespoons packed brown sugar

1 teaspoon Dijon mustard

1 cup apple cider or apple juice

• •

1. Preheat oven to 325°F. Combine garlic, salt, rosemary, thyme and pepper in small bowl. Cut lengthwise down roast almost to, but not through, bottom. Open like a book. Rub half of garlic mixture onto cut sides of pork.

2. Melt butter in large skillet over medium-high heat. Add apples and onion; cook and stir 5 to 10 minutes or until tender. Stir in brown sugar and mustard. Spread mixture evenly onto one cut side of roast. Close halves; tie roast with kitchen string at 2-inch intervals. Place roast on rack in shallow roasting pan. Pour apple cider over roast. Rub outside of roast with remaining garlic mixture.

3. Roast pork, uncovered, 2 to 2½ hours or until instant-read thermometer inserted into thickest part of roast registers 145°F, basting frequently with pan drippings. Let stand 15 minutes before slicing. (Internal temperature will continue to rise 5°F to 10°F).

TURKEY WITH SPICY CHORIZO STUFFING
Makes about 12 servings

TURKEY

- 1 whole turkey (about 14 pounds), thawed if frozen
- 1 teaspoon chili powder
- ½ teaspoon salt
- ½ teaspoon garlic powder
- ½ teaspoon dried oregano
- ¼ teaspoon black pepper
- 2 tablespoons vegetable oil

STUFFING

- 1 cup chopped pecans
- 12 ounces chorizo sausage, casings removed and crumbled
- 1½ cups thinly sliced celery
- 1 onion, chopped
- 1 red bell pepper, chopped
- 1 package (12 ounces) herb seasoned or corn bread stuffing mix
- 2 cups chicken broth
- ⅓ cup butter, cut into pieces
- 1 teaspoon dried thyme

• •

1. Preheat oven to 325°F. Remove neck and giblets from turkey; discard or reserve for another use. Place turkey breast side up on rack in large roasting pan. Pat turkey dry.

2. Combine chili powder, salt, garlic powder, oregano and black pepper in small bowl. Rub oil all over turkey and sprinkle evenly with spice mixture. Roast 3 hours or until instant-read thermometer inserted into thickest part of thigh registers 165°F (cover turkey with foil if browning too quickly). Cover and let stand 15 minutes before carving.

3. Meanwhile, heat large skillet over medium-high heat. Add pecans; cook and stir 3 minutes or just until fragrant. Spread on plate to cool.

4. Add chorizo, celery, onion and bell pepper to same skillet; cook and stir over medium-high heat 4 minutes or until chorizo is browned and vegetables are tender. Add stuffing mix, broth, butter, thyme and pecans; stir until blended.

5. Spray 13×9-inch baking dish with cooking spray; add stuffing mixture. Cover with foil; add to oven during last 40 minutes of roasting time. Let turkey stand at least 20 minutes before carving. Serve with stuffing.

HOLIDAY PORK CROWN ROAST
Makes 8 to 12 servings

ROAST

- 1 pork crown roast (about 7 pounds), thawed if frozen
- 2 tablespoons minced garlic
- 1 tablespoon dried rosemary
- 1 teaspoon salt
- ½ teaspoon black pepper
- 2 tablespoons all-purpose flour
- 1 can (about 14 ounces) chicken broth

STUFFING

- ½ cup (1 stick) butter
- 1 large onion, finely chopped
- 2 teaspoons minced garlic
- ½ teaspoon black pepper
- 2 Gala or other tart apples, peeled and finely diced (3 cups)
- 1 can (about 14 ounces) chicken broth
- 1¼ cups water
- 1 package (12 ounces) corn bread stuffing mix
- 1 cup coarsely chopped walnuts

• •

1. For roast, preheat oven to 325°F. Spray roasting pan with nonstick cooking spray. Place roast, bone side up, in pan. Cover bone tips with strips of foil. Combine garlic, rosemary, salt and ½ teaspoon pepper in small bowl. Rub mixture over entire surface of roast.

2. Place meat thermometer in middle of roast, not touching bones. Roast 2 hours. Remove foil; continue roasting 45 to 60 minutes more or until instant-read thermometer registers 155°F. Transfer to another pan; tent with foil. Let stand 15 to 20 minutes. Temperature will continue to rise to 160°F. Remove twine or netting if tied.

3. For gravy, place pan on one or two burners on stovetop. Stir flour into drippings, scraping up browned bits. Whisk in broth; cook and stir over medium heat until mixture is smooth and bubbly. Stir in any additional juices from standing roast. Strain gravy, if desired; keep warm over low heat.

4. For stuffing, melt butter in large saucepan. Add onion, garlic and ½ teaspoon pepper; cook 5 minutes or until onions are tender, stirring occasionally. Add apple; cook and stir 5 minutes. Add broth and water; bring to a simmer. Remove from heat; stir in stuffing mix and pecans. Cover; let stand 5 minutes. Fluff with fork; keep warm.

5. Transfer roast to serving platter. Place small amount of stuffing in center of rib bones. Serve with remaining stuffing and gravy.

Make Ahead

Stuffing may be prepared up to one day before serving. Coat 1½-quart baking dish with nonstick cooking spray. Spoon stuffing into dish. Cover tightly with foil and store in the refrigerator. Let stand at room temperature 30 minutes before heating. Add a little bit of broth or water if stuffing seems dry. Bake in 350°F oven for 20 to 25 minutes or until heated through.

TURKEY WITH SAUSAGE STUFFING

Makes 10 servings

1 pound bulk pork sausage

1½ cups chopped onions

1 cup chopped celery

1 clove garlic, minced

1 bag (12 ounces) herb seasoned or corn bread stuffing mix

1 can (about 14 ounces) chicken broth

2 teaspoons poultry seasoning

1 whole turkey (14 to 16 pounds), thawed if frozen

2 tablespoons butter, melted

Salt and black pepper

• •

1. Preheat oven to 325°F. Brown sausage in large skillet over medium heat 6 to 8 minutes, stirring to break up meat. Drain fat. Add onions, celery and garlic to same skillet; cook and stir over medium-high 5 minutes or until vegetables are tender. Stir in stuffing mix, broth and poultry seasoning until blended.

2. Spoon stuffing into turkey; close with metal skewers. Place turkey, breast side up, on rack in shallow roasting pan. Brush butter over outside of turkey; season with salt and pepper.

3. Roast 3 hours or until instant-read thermometer inserted into thickest part of thigh registers 165°F, basting occasionally with pan drippings. Cover and let stand 20 minutes before removing stuffing and carving turkey.

Note

If the turkey is browning too quickly,
tent loosely with foil.

BEEF TENDERLOIN WITH ROASTED VEGETABLES

Makes 10 servings

1 beef tenderloin roast (about 3 pounds), trimmed of fat

½ cup dry white wine

½ cup reduced-sodium soy sauce

2 cloves garlic, sliced

1 tablespoon fresh rosemary leaves

1 tablespoon Dijon mustard

1 teaspoon dry mustard

1 pound small red or white potatoes, cut into 1-inch pieces

1 pound Brussels sprouts, trimmed

1 package (12 ounces) baby carrots

● ●

1. Place roast in large resealable food storage bag; add wine, soy sauce, garlic, rosemary, Dijon mustard and dry mustard. Seal bag; turn to coat. Marinate in refrigerator 4 to 12 hours, turning several times.

2. Preheat oven to 425°F. Spray 13×9-inch baking pan with nonstick cooking spray. Combine potatoes, Brussels sprouts and carrots in pan. Remove roast from marinade. Pour marinade over vegetables; stir to coat. Cover with foil.

3. Roast 30 minutes. Stir vegetables; place beef on top. Roast, uncovered, 35 to 45 minutes or until beef is 135°F for medium rare to 150°F for medium.

4. Transfer tenderloin to cutting board; tent with foil. Let stand 10 to 15 minutes before slicing. (Internal temperature will continue to rise 5° to 10°F during stand time.) Reserve drippings from pan to make gravy, if desired.

5. Stir vegetables; continue roasting if not tender. Slice tenderloin; serve with roasted vegetables.

CRANBERRY-GLAZED HAM

Makes 10 to 12 servings

1 fully cooked spiral-sliced ham half (5 to 6 pounds)*

¾ cup cranberry sauce or cranberry chutney

¼ cup Dijon mustard

1 teaspoon ground cinnamon

¼ teaspoon ground allspice

A whole ham is usually about 12 pounds. Double glaze ingredients if using a whole ham.

1. Preheat oven to 300°F. Line large roasting pan with foil. Place ham in pan. Combine cranberry sauce, mustard, cinnamon and allspice in medium bowl; stir until well blended. Spread half of mixture evenly over top of ham. (Glaze will melt and spread as it cooks.)

2. Bake 1 hour; spread remaining cranberry mixture over top of ham. Bake about 1 hour or until internal temperature reaches 140°F. Transfer ham to cutting board; let stand 5 minutes before slicing.

Down-Home Holiday Menu

Classic Deviled Eggs, page 16

Cranberry-Glazed Ham

Sweet Potato and Pecan Casserole, page 112

Green Bean, Walnut and Blue Cheese Pasta Salad, page 96

Roasted Garlic Mac and Cheese, page 114

Simple Golden Corn Bread, page 140

Carrot Cake, page 154

SALADS
ON THE SIDE

KALE SALAD WITH CHERRIES AND AVOCADOS
Makes 6 to 8 servings

¼ cup plus 1 teaspoon olive oil, divided

3 tablespoons uncooked quinoa

¾ teaspoon salt, divided

3 tablespoons balsamic vinegar

1 tablespoon red wine vinegar

1 tablespoon maple syrup

2 teaspoons Dijon mustard

¼ teaspoon dried oregano

⅛ teaspoon black pepper

1 large bunch kale (about 1 pound)

1 package (5 ounces) dried cherries

2 avocados, diced

½ cup smoked almonds, chopped

• •

1. Heat 1 teaspoon oil in small saucepan over medium-high heat. Add quinoa; cook and stir 3 to 5 minutes or until quinoa is golden brown and popped. Season with ¼ teaspoon salt. Remove to plate; cool completely.

2. Combine balsamic vinegar, red wine vinegar, maple syrup, mustard, oregano, pepper and remaining ½ teaspoon salt in medium bowl. Whisk in remaining ¼ cup oil until well blended.

3. Place kale in large bowl. Pour dressing over kale; massage dressing into leaves until well blended and kale is slightly softened. Add popped quinoa; stir until well blended. Add cherries, avocados and almonds; toss until blended.

SPINACH, ORANGE AND FETA SALAD
Makes 8 to 10 servings

DRESSING

- ¼ cup balsamic vinegar
- 1 clove garlic, minced
- ½ teaspoon sugar
- ¼ teaspoon salt
- ⅛ teaspoon black pepper
- ¼ cup olive oil
- ¼ cup vegetable oil

SALAD

- 8 cups packed baby spinach
- 1 cup diced tomatoes (about 2 medium)
- 1 cup drained mandarin oranges

- 1 cup glazed pecans*
- ½ cup crumbled feta cheese
- ½ cup diced red onion
- ½ cup dried cranberries
- 1 can (3 ounces) crispy rice noodles**
- 4 teaspoons toasted sesame seeds

Glazed pecans can be found in the produce section of large supermarkets with other salad toppings or in the baking aisle. If unavailable, make them at home (recipe follows).

**Crispy rice noodles can be found with canned chow mein noodles in the Asian section of the supermarket.*

• •

1. For dressing, whisk vinegar, garlic, sugar, salt and pepper in medium bowl until blended. Slowly whisk in olive oil and vegetable oil in thin, steady stream until well blended.

2. For salad, combine spinach, tomatoes, oranges, pecans, cheese, onion and cranberries in large bowl. Sprinkle with rice noodles and sesame seeds. Add dressing; toss to mix.

Glazed Pecans

To make glazed pecans, combine 1 cup pecan halves, ¼ cup sugar, 1 tablespoon butter and ½ teaspoon salt in medium skillet; cook and stir over medium heat 5 minutes or until sugar mixture is dark brown and nuts are well coated. Spread on large plate; cool completely. Break into pieces or coarsely chop.

ROASTED BRUSSELS SPROUTS SALAD
Makes 8 to 10 servings

BRUSSELS SPROUTS

- 1 pound Brussels sprouts, trimmed and halved
- 2 tablespoons olive oil
- ½ teaspoon salt

SALAD

- 2 cups coarsely chopped baby kale
- 2 cups coarsely chopped romaine lettuce
- 1½ cups glazed pecans*
- 1 cup halved red grapes
- 1 cup diced cucumbers
- ½ cup dried cranberries
- ½ cup fresh blueberries
- ½ cup chopped red onion
- ¼ cup toasted pumpkin seeds (pepitas)
- 1 container (4 ounces) crumbled goat cheese

DRESSING

- ½ cup olive oil
- 6 tablespoons balsamic vinegar
- 6 tablespoons strawberry jam
- 2 teaspoons Dijon mustard
- 1 teaspoon salt

*Glazed pecans can be found in the produce section of large supermarkets with other salad toppings or in the baking aisle. If unavailable, make them yourself (recipe page 80).

● ●

1. For Brussels sprouts, preheat oven to 400°F. Spray large baking sheet with nonstick cooking spray.

2. Combine Brussels sprouts, 2 tablespoons oil and ½ teaspoon salt in medium bowl; toss to coat. Arrange Brussels sprouts in single layer, cut sides down, on prepared baking sheet. Roast 20 minutes or until tender and browned, stirring once halfway through roasting. Cool completely on baking sheet.

3. For salad, combine kale, lettuce, pecans, grapes, cucumbers, cranberries, blueberries, onion and pumpkin seeds in large bowl. Top with Brussels sprouts and cheese.

4. For dressing, whisk ½ cup oil, vinegar, jam, mustard and 1 teaspoon salt in small bowl until well blended. Pour dressing over salad; toss gently to coat.

BROCCOLI AND CAULIFLOWER SALAD
Makes 8 servings

1 package (about 12 ounces) bacon, chopped

2 cups mayonnaise

¼ cup sugar

¼ cup white or apple cider vinegar

4 cups chopped raw broccoli

4 cups coarsely chopped raw cauliflower

1½ cups (6 ounces) shredded Cheddar cheese

1 cup chopped red onion

1 cup dried cranberries or raisins (optional)

½ cup sunflower seeds (optional)

Salt and black pepper

• •

1. Cook bacon in large skillet over medium heat until crisp, stirring frequently. Remove from skillet with slotted spoon; drain on paper towel-lined plate.

2. Whisk mayonnaise, sugar and vinegar in large bowl. Stir in broccoli, cauliflower, cheese, onion and cranberries, if desired; mix well. Fold in bacon and sunflower seeds, if desired. Season with salt and pepper.

3. Serve immediately or cover and refrigerate until ready to serve.

PEAR ARUGULA SALAD
Makes 4 servings

CARAMELIZED PECANS

- ½ cup pecan halves
- 3 tablespoons packed brown sugar
- 1 tablespoon butter
- 1 tablespoon honey
- ¼ teaspoon salt
- ⅛ teaspoon ground cinnamon

DRESSING

- ¼ cup olive oil
- 3 tablespoons balsamic vinegar
- 1 teaspoon pomegranate molasses or honey
- 1 teaspoon Dijon mustard
- ½ teaspoon salt
- ¼ teaspoon dried thyme
- ⅛ teaspoon black pepper

SALAD

- 2 cups arugula
- 2 red pears, thinly sliced
- ½ cup crumbled gorgonzola, blue or goat cheese

• •

1. Preheat oven to 350°F. Line small baking sheet with foil; spray foil with nonstick cooking spray. Combine pecans, brown sugar, butter, honey, ¼ teaspoon salt and cinnamon in medium skillet. Cook and stir 2 to 3 minutes or until nuts are glazed. Spread on foil. Bake 5 to 7 minutes or until nuts are fragrant and a shade darker. Slide nuts on foil onto wire rack; cool completely.

2. For dressing, whisk oil, vinegar, molasses, mustard, ½ teaspoon salt, thyme and pepper in small bowl until smooth and well blended.

3. Place arugula in medium serving bowl. Top with pears, nuts and cheese. Add dressing; toss to coat.

CHOPPED SALAD
Makes 12 to 14 servings

DRESSING

⅓ cup white balsamic vinegar

¼ cup Dijon mustard

1 package (about 2 tablespoons) Italian salad dressing mix

⅔ cup olive oil

SALAD

1 medium head iceberg lettuce, chopped

1 medium head romaine lettuce, chopped

1 can (about 14 ounces) hearts of palm or artichoke hearts, quartered lengthwise then sliced crosswise

1 large avocado, diced

1½ cups crumbled blue cheese

2 hard-cooked eggs, chopped

1 ripe tomato, chopped

½ small red onion, finely chopped

1 package (about 12 ounces) bacon, crisp-cooked and crumbled

● ●

1. For dressing, whisk vinegar, mustard and dressing mix in small bowl. Slowly add oil, whisking until well blended. Set aside until ready to use. (Dressing can be made up to 1 week in advance; refrigerate in jar with tight-fitting lid and shake to blend before using.)

2. For salad, combine lettuce, hearts of palm, avocado, cheese, eggs, tomato, onion and bacon in large bowl. Add dressing; toss to coat.

Tip

If there isn't room on your table for a salad, make it an appetizer. Portion salad into paper cups, short wide-mouth jars or even juice glasses and set it out with your snacks and cheeseball (or assign a kid or party guest to walk around and pass it out).

FARRO, CHICKPEA AND SPINACH SALAD
Makes 6 servings

1 cup uncooked pearled farro

3 cups baby spinach, stemmed

1 medium cucumber, chopped

1 can (about 15 ounces) chickpeas, rinsed and drained

¾ cup pitted kalamata olives

¼ cup olive oil

3 tablespoons white or golden balsamic vinegar *or* 3 tablespoons cider vinegar mixed with ½ teaspoon sugar

1 teaspoon chopped fresh rosemary

1 clove garlic, minced

1 teaspoon salt

⅛ to ¼ teaspoon red pepper flakes (optional)

½ cup crumbled goat or feta cheese

• •

1. Bring 4 cups water to a boil in medium saucepan. Add farro; reduce heat and simmer 20 to 25 minutes or until farro is tender. Drain and rinse under cold water until cool.

2. Meanwhile, combine spinach, cucumber, chickpeas, olives, oil, vinegar, rosemary, garlic, salt and red pepper flakes, if desired, in large bowl. Stir in farro until well blended. Add cheese; stir gently. Salad can be made a day in advance.

MESCLUN SALAD WITH CRANBERRY VINAIGRETTE
Makes 8 servings

DRESSING

- ⅓ cup olive oil
- 3 tablespoons champagne vinegar or sherry vinegar
- 1 tablespoon Dijon mustard
- ¾ teaspoon salt
- ¼ teaspoon black pepper
- ½ cup dried cranberries

SALAD

- 10 cups (10 ounces) mesclun or mixed torn salad greens
- 4 ounces goat cheese, crumbled
- ½ cup walnuts or pecans, coarsely chopped and toasted*

*To toast walnuts, cook in medium skillet over medium heat 3 to 4 minutes or until lightly browned and fragrant, stirring frequently.

● ●

1. For dressing, whisk oil, vinegar, mustard, salt and pepper in small bowl. Stir in cranberries. Cover; refrigerate at least 30 minutes or up to 24 hours before serving.

2. For salad, combine salad greens, goat cheese and walnuts in large bowl. Whisk dressing again and add to salad; toss until evenly coated.

Small and Simple Feast

Leek Strudels, page 22

Pear Arugula Salad, page 86

Simple Roasted Chicken, page 56

Brussels Sprouts with Honey Butter, page 100

Old-Fashioned Herb Stuffing, page 108

Cinnamon Plum Walnut Cobbler, page 152

CRUNCHY CARROT CRANBERRY SLAW
Makes 6 to 8 servings

4 cups shredded carrots*

2 packages (3 ounces each) ramen noodles, crumbled**

½ cup chopped walnuts

½ cup dried cranberries

¼ cup chopped green onions

¼ cup mayonnaise

2 tablespoons packed brown sugar

2 teaspoons lime juice

1 teaspoon honey

Salt and black pepper

For convenience, purchase a 10-ounce package of shredded carrots.

**Use any flavor; discard seasoning packet.*

• •

1. Combine carrots, noodles, walnuts, cranberries and green onions in large bowl. Whisk mayonnaise, brown sugar, lime juice and honey in medium bowl; season with salt and pepper. Stir into carrot mixture until well blended.

2. Refrigerate until ready to serve.

GREEN BEAN, WALNUT AND BLUE CHEESE PASTA SALAD
Makes 8 servings

- 2 cups uncooked gemelli pasta
- 2 cups trimmed halved green beans
- 3 tablespoons olive oil
- 2 tablespoons white wine vinegar
- 1 tablespoon chopped fresh thyme
- 1 tablespoon Dijon mustard
- 1 tablespoon fresh lemon juice

- 1 teaspoon honey
- ¼ teaspoon salt
- ¼ teaspoon black pepper
- ½ cup chopped walnuts, toasted*
- ½ cup crumbled blue cheese

To toast walnuts, cook in medium skillet over medium heat 3 to 4 minutes or until lightly browned and fragrant, stirring frequently.

• •

1. Cook pasta in large saucepan of salted boiling water according to package directions for al dente. Add green beans during last 4 minutes of cooking. Drain and place in large bowl.

2. Meanwhile, whisk oil, vinegar, thyme, mustard, lemon juice, honey, salt and pepper in medium bowl until smooth and well blended.

3. Pour dressing over pasta and green beans; toss to coat evenly. Stir in walnuts and cheese. Serve warm or cover and refrigerate until ready to serve.**

Stir walnuts into salad just before serving.

VEGETABLES & SIDES

BRUSSELS SPROUTS WITH HONEY BUTTER
Makes 4 servings

6 slices thick-cut bacon,
    cut into ½-inch pieces

1½ pounds Brussels sprouts
    (about 24 medium), halved

¼ teaspoon salt

¼ teaspoon black pepper

2 tablespoons butter, softened

2 tablespoons honey

• •

1. Preheat oven to 375°F. Cook bacon in medium skillet until almost crisp. Drain on paper towel-lined plate; set aside. Reserve 1 tablespoon drippings.

2. Place Brussels sprouts on large baking sheet. Drizzle with reserved bacon drippings and sprinkle with ¼ teaspoon salt and ¼ teaspoon pepper; toss to coat. Arrange Brussels sprouts in single layer, cut sides down, on prepared baking sheet. Roast 30 minutes or until tender and browned, stirring once halfway through roasting.

3. Roast 30 minutes or until Brussels sprouts are browned, stirring once.

4. Combine butter and honey in medium bowl; mix well. Add Brussels sprouts; stir until completely coated. Stir in bacon; season with additional salt and pepper.

RED CABBAGE WITH BACON AND MUSHROOMS
Makes 6 servings

8 ounces thick-cut bacon, chopped

1 onion, chopped

1 package (8 ounces) cremini mushrooms, cut into ½-inch pieces

¾ teaspoon dried thyme

½ medium red cabbage, cut into wedges, cored and cut crosswise into ¼-inch slices (about 7 cups)

¼ teaspoon salt

¼ teaspoon black pepper

⅔ cup chicken broth

3 tablespoons cider vinegar

¼ cup chopped walnuts, toasted*

3 tablespoons chopped fresh parsley

*To toast walnuts, cook in small skillet over medium heat 4 to 5 minutes or until lightly browned, stirring frequently.

• •

1. Cook bacon in large saucepan or skillet over medium-high heat until crisp. Remove to paper towel-lined plate. Drain all but 1 tablespoon drippings from saucepan.

2. Add onion to same saucepan; cook and stir 5 minutes or until softened. Add mushrooms and thyme; cook 6 minutes or until mushrooms begin to brown, stirring occasionally. Add cabbage, ¼ teaspoon salt and ¼ teaspoon pepper; cook and stir 7 minutes or until cabbage is wilted.

3. Stir in broth, vinegar and half of bacon; bring to a boil. Reduce heat to low; cook, uncovered, 15 to 20 minutes or until cabbage is tender.

4. Stir in walnuts and parsley; season with additional salt and pepper, if desired. Sprinkle with remaining bacon.

PARMESAN ALFREDO PASTA BAKE
Makes 6 to 8 servings

1 package (16 ounces) uncooked fusilli pasta

6 tablespoons butter

1 clove garlic

½ teaspoon salt

1 cup whipping cream

1 cup milk

2 cups shredded Parmesan cheese, divided

1 cup (4 ounces) shredded mozzarella cheese

4 ounces mozzarella cheese, cubed

1 cup panko bread crumbs

2 tablespoons butter, melted

¼ teaspoon Italian seasoning

• •

1. Preheat oven to 400°F. Spray 3-quart baking dish with nonstick cooking spray.

2. Cook pasta in large saucepan of salted boiling water according to package directions for al dente. Drain pasta, reserving ½ cup cooking water. Return pasta to saucepan.

3. Meanwhile, melt 6 tablespoons butter in medium saucepan over medium heat. Add garlic and salt. Stir in cream, milk and ½ cup pasta water; bring to a simmer. Remove from heat; remove and discard garlic clove. Gradually stir in 1 cup Parmesan and shredded mozzarella until smooth and well blended. Pour over pasta; stir gently to coat. Pour into prepared baking dish; fold in cubed mozzarella.

4. Combine panko, remaining 1 cup Parmesan and 2 tablespoons melted butter in medium bowl. Spread evenly over pasta mixture; sprinkle with Italian seasoning.

5. Bake 15 minutes or until topping is golden brown and pasta is heated through.

GREEN BEANS GREMOLATA
Makes 8 servings

2 pounds fresh green beans, trimmed

3 tablespoons olive oil

½ cup grated Parmesan cheese

⅓ cup chopped fresh parsley

2 tablespoons grated lemon peel

3 cloves garlic, minced

Salt and black pepper

1. Bring large pot of salted water to a boil. Add green beans; cook 3 minutes or until crisp-tender. Drain and place in large bowl. Add oil; toss to coat.

2. Combine Parmesan, parsley, lemon peel and garlic in medium bowl; season to taste with salt and pepper. Pour over green beans; toss gently to coat.

Classic Thanksgiving Menu

Baked Brie with Nut Crust, page 44

Mini Spinach and Bacon Quiches, page 12

Turkey with Apple Corn Bread Stuffing, page 60

Roasted Brussels Sprouts Salad, page 82

Green Bean Casserole with Homemade French Fried Onions, page 118

Sour Cream Mashed Potatoes, page 122

Orange Glazed Carrots, page 116

Cinnamon Ginger Pumpkin Pie, page 158

OLD-FASHIONED HERB STUFFING
Makes 4 servings

6 slices (8 ounces) whole wheat, rye or white bread (or a combination), cut into ½-inch cubes

1 tablespoon butter

1 cup chopped onion

½ cup thinly sliced celery

½ cup thinly sliced carrot

1 cup vegetable broth

1 tablespoon chopped fresh thyme *or* 1 teaspoon dried thyme

1 tablespoon chopped fresh sage *or* 1 teaspoon dried sage

½ teaspoon paprika

¼ teaspoon black pepper

1. Preheat oven to 350°F. Spray 1½-quart baking dish with nonstick cooking spray.

2. Place bread cubes on baking sheet; bake 10 minutes or until dry.

3. Melt butter in large saucepan over medium heat. Add onion, celery and carrot; cook and stir 10 minutes or until vegetables are tender. Add broth, thyme, sage, paprika and pepper; bring to a simmer. Stir in bread cubes. Spoon into prepared baking dish.

4. Cover and bake 25 to 30 minutes or until heated through.

CINNAMON APPLES
Makes 6 servings

¼ cup (½ stick) butter

3 tart red apples such as Gala, Fuji or Honeycrisp (about 1½ pounds total), peeled and cut into ½-inch wedges

¼ cup packed brown sugar

1 teaspoon ground cinnamon

⅛ teaspoon ground nutmeg

⅛ teaspoon salt

1 tablespoon cornstarch

• •

1. Melt butter in large skillet over medium-high heat. Add apples; cook 8 minutes or until tender, stirring occasionally.

2. Add brown sugar, cinnamon, nutmeg and salt; cook and stir 1 minute or until apples are glazed. Reduce heat to medium-low; stir in cornstarch until well blended.

3. Remove from heat; let stand 5 minutes for glaze to thicken. Stir again; serve immediately.

SWEET POTATO AND PECAN CASSEROLE

Makes 6 to 8 servings

1 can (40 ounces) sweet
    potatoes, drained

½ cup apple juice

⅓ cup plus 2 tablespoons butter,
    melted, divided

½ teaspoon salt

½ teaspoon ground cinnamon

¼ teaspoon black pepper

2 eggs

⅓ cup chopped pecans

⅓ cup packed brown sugar

2 tablespoons all-purpose flour

• •

Slow Cooker Directions

1. Lightly grease slow cooker. Mash sweet potatoes in large bowl. Stir in apple juice, ⅓ cup butter, salt, cinnamon and pepper. Add eggs; beat until blended. Place mixture into prepared slow cooker.

2. Combine pecans, brown sugar, flour and remaining 2 tablespoons butter in small bowl. Spread over sweet potatoes.

3. Cover; cook on HIGH 3 to 4 hours.

Tip

This casserole is excellent to make for
the holidays. Using the slow cooker frees
the oven for other dishes.

ROASTED GARLIC MAC AND CHEESE
Makes 8 to 10 servings

6 tablespoons butter, divided, plus additional for baking dish

1 head garlic

1 tablespoon olive oil

1¼ teaspoons salt, divided

1 cup panko bread crumbs

1 package (16 ounces) cellentani pasta*

¼ cup all-purpose flour

½ teaspoon black pepper

2 cups whole milk

¾ cup Irish stout

2 cups (8 ounces) shredded sharp Cheddar cheese

2 cups (8 ounces) shredded Dubliner or white Cheddar cheese

Or substitute elbow macaroni, penne or other favorite pasta shape.

• •

1. Preheat oven to 375°F. Butter 4-quart shallow baking dish.

2. Place garlic on 10-inch piece of foil; drizzle with oil and crimp shut. Place on small baking sheet; bake 30 minutes or until tender. Cool 15 minutes; squeeze cloves into small bowl. Mash into smooth paste.

3. Meanwhile, melt 2 tablespoons butter in medium saucepan over medium heat until melted. Stir in ¼ teaspoon salt until dissolved. Stir in panko until well blended.

4. Cook pasta in large saucepan of salted boiling water according to package directions for al dente. Drain and return to saucepan.

5. Melt remaining 4 tablespoons butter in large saucepan over medium heat. Add flour; cook and stir until lightly browned. Stir in garlic paste, remaining 1 teaspoon salt and pepper. Slowly whisk in milk and stout; cook until thickened, whisking constantly. Remove from heat; add cheese by ½ cupfuls, stirring until cheese is melted before adding each addition. Add pasta; stir until coated. Spoon into prepared baking dish; sprinkle with panko mixture.

6. Bake 40 minutes or until bubbly and topping is golden brown. Let stand 10 minutes before serving.

ORANGE GLAZED CARROTS
Makes 6 servings

1 package (32 ounces) baby carrots

1 tablespoon packed brown sugar

1 tablespoon orange juice

1 tablespoon melted butter

¼ teaspoon ground cinnamon

⅛ teaspoon ground nutmeg

Salt and black pepper

Orange peel (optional)

1. Bring 1 inch lightly salted water in 2-quart saucepan to a boil over high heat; add carrots. Return to a boil. Reduce heat to low; cover and simmer 10 to 12 minutes or until crisp-tender. Drain well; return carrots to saucepan.

2. Stir in brown sugar, orange juice, butter, cinnamon and nutmeg. Cook 3 minutes or until carrots are glazed, stirring occasionally. Season to taste with salt and pepper. Garnish with orange peel, if desired.

GREEN BEAN CASSEROLE WITH HOMEMADE FRENCH FRIED ONIONS
Makes 6 to 8 servings

1 pound fresh green beans, cut into 2-inch pieces

1 tablespoon vegetable oil

8 ounces cremini mushrooms, chopped

3 tablespoons butter

3 tablespoons all-purpose flour

1 teaspoon salt

¼ teaspoon red pepper flakes

1 cup mushroom or vegetable broth

1 cup whole milk

Homemade French Fried Onions (page 119)

• •

1. Preheat oven to 350°F. Spray 13×9-inch baking dish with nonstick cooking spray.

2. Cook green beans in large saucepan of salted boiling water 4 minutes. Drain.

3. Heat oil in large saucepan over medium heat. Add mushrooms; cook and stir 8 minutes. Add butter; cook and stir until melted. Whisk in flour, salt and red pepper flakes. Gradually whisk in broth and milk; cook and stir until thickened. Remove from heat; stir in green beans. Pour into prepared dish.

4. Bake 30 minutes. Meanwhile, prepare Homemade French Fried Onions.*

5. Remove casserole from oven. Top with onions; bake 5 minutes.

Onions can be made a day in advance. Drain thoroughly and cool completely; store in a tightly covered container at room temperature.

Tip

Double or triple the recipe for Homemade French Fried Onions and serve them as part of your appetizer spread. They go particularly well with Lemony Ranch Dip (page 48) and Three-Cheese Roasted Garlic Spread (page 50).

HOMEMADE FRENCH FRIED ONIONS
Makes about 1½ cups

2 small onions, sliced into rings

½ cup milk

½ cup cornstarch

½ cup cornmeal

1 teaspoon salt

½ teaspoon black pepper

Vegetable oil for frying

● ●

1. Line baking sheet with paper towels. Separate onion rings and spread in shallow dish. Pour milk over onions; stir to coat. Combine cornstarch, cornmeal, salt and pepper in large bowl.

2. Heat 2 inches of oil in large heavy skillet over medium-high heat to 325°F on deep-fry thermometer.

3. Working in batches, remove onion rings from milk to cornmeal mixture; toss to coat. Add onions to oil; fry 2 minutes per side or until golden brown. Remove to prepared baking sheet using slotted spoon or tongs.

ROASTED CAULIFLOWER WITH CHEDDAR BEER SAUCE

Makes 4 to 6 servings (1¼ cups sauce)

1 large head cauliflower (about 2½ pounds), trimmed and cut into ½-inch florets

2 tablespoons vegetable oil, divided

½ teaspoon salt, divided

½ teaspoon black pepper

2 shallots, finely chopped

2 teaspoons all-purpose flour

½ cup Irish ale*

1 tablespoon spicy brown mustard

1 tablespoon Worcestershire sauce

1½ cups (6 ounces) shredded Cheddar cheese

*Or substitute your favorite beer, milk or vegetable broth.

• •

1. Preheat oven to 450°F. Line large baking sheet with foil.

2. Combine cauliflower, 1 tablespoon oil, ¼ teaspoon salt and pepper in medium bowl; toss to coat. Spread in single layer on prepared baking sheet.

3. Roast 25 minutes or until tender and lightly browned, stirring once.

4. Meanwhile for sauce, heat remaining 1 tablespoon oil in medium saucepan over medium-high heat. Add shallots; cook and stir 3 to 4 minutes or until tender. Add flour and remaining ¼ teaspoon salt; cook and stir 1 minute. Gradually whisk in ale until mixture is smooth. Stir in mustard and Worcestershire sauce; bring to a simmer. Reduce heat to medium-low; add cheese by ¼ cupfuls, stirring until cheese is melted before adding next addition. Cover and keep warm over low heat, stirring occasionally.

5. Transfer roasted cauliflower to large serving bowl; top with cheese sauce. Serve immediately.

Tip

Try serving this sauce over any roasted vegetable, or as an appetizer with toasted French bread slices and/or raw broccoli florets for dipping.

SOUR CREAM GARLIC MASHED POTATOES

Makes 10 to 12 servings

5 pounds red potatoes, peeled*
   and cut into 1-inch pieces

8 cloves garlic, peeled

½ cup (1 stick) butter, softened

1½ cups sour cream

2 teaspoons salt

½ teaspoon white pepper

For more texture, leave the potatoes unpeeled.

• •

1. Place potatoes and garlic in large saucepan; cover with water. Bring to a boil over high heat. Reduce heat to low; simmer 20 minutes or until potatoes are tender. Drain.

2. Return potatoes to saucepan. Add butter; mash with potato masher until smooth and butter is melted. Stir in sour cream, salt and pepper until well blended.

Classic Irish Champ

Irish Champ is a traditional dish of mashed potatoes with
green onions (champ means "pound" or "smash"). Omit the garlic
and stir in 1 cup chopped green onions with the sour cream.
Top each serving with a pat of additional butter.

POTATO AND LEEK GRATIN
Makes 6 to 8 servings

5 tablespoons butter, divided

2 large leeks, sliced

2 tablespoons minced garlic

2 pounds baking potatoes, peeled (about 4 medium)

1 cup whipping cream

1 cup milk

3 eggs

2 teaspoons salt

¼ teaspoon white pepper

2 to 3 slices dense day-old white bread, such as French or Italian

½ cup grated Parmesan cheese

• •

1. Preheat oven to 375°F. Generously grease shallow 2½-quart baking dish with 1 tablespoon butter.

2. Melt 2 tablespoons butter in large skillet over medium heat. Add leeks and garlic; cook and stir 8 to 10 minutes or until leeks are softened. Remove from heat.

3. Cut potatoes crosswise into 1⁄16-inch-thick slices. Layer half of potato slices in prepared baking dish; top with half of leek mixture. Repeat layers. Whisk cream, milk, eggs, salt and pepper in medium bowl until well blended; pour evenly over leek mixture.

4. Tear bread slices into 1-inch pieces. Place in food processor or blender; process until fine crumbs form. Measure ¾ cup crumbs; place in small bowl. Stir in cheese. Melt remaining 2 tablespoons butter; stir into crumb mixture. Sprinkle over vegetables in baking dish.

5. Bake 1 hour 15 minutes or until top is golden brown and potatoes are tender. Let stand 5 to 10 minutes before serving.

BUTTERNUT SQUASH IN COCONUT MILK
Makes 4 to 6 servings

⅓ cup flaked coconut

2 teaspoons vegetable oil

½ small onion, finely chopped

2 cloves garlic, minced

1 cup unsweetened coconut milk

¼ cup packed brown sugar

1 tablespoon fish sauce or soy sauce

¼ teaspoon salt

⅛ to ¼ teaspoon red pepper flakes

1 butternut squash (2 to 2½ pounds), peeled and cut into 1-inch cubes

1 tablespoon chopped fresh cilantro

• •

1. Preheat oven to 350°F. Cook coconut in medium skillet over medium-low heat 5 to 7 minutes or until toasted, stirring frequently. Spread on plate; cool completely.

2. Heat oil in large saucepan over medium-high heat. Add onion and garlic; cook and stir 3 minutes or until tender. Add coconut milk, brown sugar, fish sauce, salt and red pepper flakes; stir until brown sugar is dissolved. Bring to a boil; stir in squash.

3. Reduce heat to medium; cover and simmer 30 minutes or until squash is tender. Transfer squash to serving bowl with slotted spoon.

4. Increase heat to high; boil remaining liquid until thick, stirring constantly. Pour liquid over squash in bowl; stir gently to blend. Sprinkle with toasted coconut and cilantro.

HOMEMADE BREADS

CHEDDAR QUICK BREAD
Makes 1 loaf

2 cups all-purpose flour

4 teaspoons baking powder

1 tablespoon sugar

½ teaspoon salt

½ teaspoon onion powder

½ teaspoon dry mustard

1½ cups (6 ounces) shredded Cheddar cheese

1 cup milk

1 egg

2 tablespoons butter, melted

• •

1. Preheat oven to 350°F. Spray 8×4-inch loaf pan with nonstick cooking spray.

2. Whisk flour, baking powder, sugar, salt, onion powder and mustard in large bowl. Stir in cheese until well blended.

3. Whisk milk, egg and butter in medium bowl until well blended. Add to flour mixture; stir just until combined. Spread batter in prepared pan.

4. Bake 40 to 45 minutes or until toothpick inserted into center comes out clean. Cool in pan 10 minutes. Remove to wire rack; serve warm or cool completely.

Tip

Serve this bread as part of an appetizer board.
Cut it into cubes and serve alongside vegetables
and crackers with Garlic and Herb Dip or
Easy Fried Onion Dip (page 46).

PESTO ROLLS
Makes 12 rolls

- 3 cups all-purpose flour, divided
- 1 package (¼ ounce) active dry yeast
- 1½ teaspoons salt
- 1 cup warm water (120°F)
- 2 tablespoons olive oil

- ½ cup pesto sauce, store bought or homemade (recipe follows)
- 1 cup (4 ounces) shredded mozzarella cheese
- ⅓ cup grated Parmesan cheese
- ¼ cup chopped drained oil-packed sun-dried tomatoes

• •

1. Combine 1½ cups flour, yeast and salt in large bowl of electric mixer. Add warm water and oil; beat at medium speed 2 minutes.

2. Add remaining 1½ cups flour; knead with dough hook at low speed 5 minutes or until dough is smooth and elastic. Shape dough into a ball. Place in greased bowl; turn to grease top. Cover and let rise in warm place about 45 minutes or until doubled in size.

3. Spray 12×8-inch baking pan with nonstick cooking spray. Turn out dough onto lightly floured surface; roll into 18×12-inch rectangle. Spread pesto evenly over dough; sprinkle with mozzarella, Parmesan and sun-dried tomatoes. Starting with long side, roll up dough jelly-roll style; pinch seam to seal. Trim ends; cut roll crosswise into 12 (1½-inch) slices. Place slices cut sides up in prepared pan; cover and let rise in warm place about 30 minutes or until rolls are puffy and almost doubled in size. Preheat oven to 350°F.

4. Bake 22 to 27 minutes or until lightly browned. Cool slightly before serving.

Pesto Sauce

Place 2 cups fresh basil leaves, ¼ cup pine nuts, ¼ cup olive oil, 3 cloves garlic, minced, and ¼ teaspoon salt in blender or food processor. Process until evenly blended and pine nuts are finely chopped. Scrape down side of bowl. Stir in ½ cup grated Parmesan cheese. Refrigerate until ready to serve (pesto can be refrigerated up to 2 weeks). Makes about 1 cup.

GARLIC KNOTS
Makes 20 knots

¾ cup warm water (105° to 115°F)

1 package (¼ ounce) active dry yeast

1 teaspoon sugar

2¼ cups all-purpose flour

2 tablespoons olive oil, divided

1½ teaspoons salt, divided

4 tablespoons (½ stick) butter, divided

1 tablespoon minced garlic

¼ teaspoon garlic powder

½ cup grated Parmesan cheese

2 tablespoons chopped fresh parsley

½ teaspoon dried oregano

• •

1. Combine warm water, yeast and sugar in large bowl of electric mixer; stir to dissolve yeast. Let stand 5 minutes or until mixture is bubbly. Stir in flour, 1 tablespoon oil and 1 teaspoon salt; knead with dough hook at low speed 5 minutes or until dough is smooth and elastic. Shape dough into a ball. Place in large greased bowl; turn to grease top. Cover and let rise 1 hour or until doubled in size.

2. Melt 2 tablespoons butter in small saucepan over low heat. Add remaining 1 tablespoon oil, ½ teaspoon salt, minced garlic and garlic powder; cook over very low heat 5 minutes. Pour into small bowl; set aside.

3. Preheat oven to 400°F. Line baking sheet with parchment paper. Turn out dough onto lightly floured surface. Punch down dough; let stand 10 minutes. Roll out dough into 10×8-inch rectangle. Cut into 20 (2-inch) squares. Roll each piece into 8-inch rope; tie in a knot. Place knots on prepared baking sheet; brush with garlic mixture.

4. Bake 10 minutes or until knots are lightly browned. Meanwhile, melt remaining 2 tablespoons butter in small saucepan or microwavable bowl. Combine cheese, parsley and oregano in small bowl; mix well. Brush melted butter over baked knots immediately after baking; sprinkle with cheese mixture. Cool slightly; serve warm.

QUATTRO FORMAGGIO FOCACCIA
Makes 12 servings

1 tablespoon sugar

1 package (¼ ounce) active dry yeast

1¼ cups warm water (105° to 115°F)

3 to 3¼ cups all-purpose flour

¼ cup plus 2 tablespoons olive oil, divided

1 teaspoon salt

¼ cup marinara sauce with basil

1 cup (4 ounces) shredded Italian cheese blend

• •

1. Dissolve sugar and yeast in warm water in large bowl of electric mixer; let stand 5 minutes or until bubbly. Stir in 3 cups flour, ¼ cup oil and salt with spoon or spatula to form rough dough. Knead with dough hook at low speed 5 minutes, adding additional flour, 1 tablespoon at a time, if necessary for dough to come together. (Dough will be sticky and will not clean side of bowl.)

2. Scrape dough into large greased bowl; turn to grease top. Cover and let rise about 1 hour or until doubled in size.

3. Punch down dough. Pour remaining 2 tablespoons oil into 13×9-inch baking pan; add dough and pat and stretch to fill pan. Make indentations in top of dough with fingertips.

4. Spread marinara sauce evenly over dough. Cover and let rise 30 minutes or until puffy. Preheat oven to 425°F.

5. Sprinkle cheese over top of dough. Bake 17 to 20 minutes or until golden brown. Cut into squares or strips.

SOFT GARLIC BREADSTICKS
Makes about 16 breadsticks

1½ cups water

6 tablespoons (¾ stick) butter, divided

4 cups all-purpose flour

2 tablespoons sugar

1 package (¼ ounce) active dry yeast

1½ teaspoons salt

¾ teaspoon coarse salt

¼ teaspoon garlic powder

• •

1. Heat water and 2 tablespoons butter in small saucepan over medium heat to 110° to 115°F. (Butter does not need to melt completely.)

2. Combine flour, sugar, yeast and 1½ teaspoons salt in large bowl of electric mixer. Add water mixture; mix with dough hook at low speed until dough begins to come together. Knead about 5 minutes or until dough is smooth and elastic. Shape dough into a ball. Place in large greased bowl; turn to grease top. Cover and let rise in warm place about 1 hour or until doubled in size.

3. Line two baking sheets with parchment paper or spray with nonstick cooking spray. Punch down dough. For each breadstick, pull off piece of dough slightly larger than a golf ball (about 2 ounces) and roll between hands or on work surface into 7-inch-long rope. Place on prepared baking sheets; cover loosely and let rise in warm place about 45 minutes or until doubled in size.

4. Preheat oven to 400°F. Melt remaining 4 tablespoons butter. Brush breadsticks with 2 tablespoons butter; sprinkle with coarse salt.

5. Bake 13 to 15 minutes or until golden brown. Stir garlic powder into remaining 2 tablespoons melted butter; brush over breadsticks immediately after removing from oven. Serve warm.

SIMPLE GOLDEN CORN BREAD
Makes 9 to 12 servings

1¼ cups all-purpose flour

¾ cup yellow cornmeal

⅓ cup sugar

2 teaspoons baking powder

1 teaspoon salt

1¼ cups whole milk

¼ cup (½ stick) butter, melted

1 egg

Honey Butter (recipe follows, optional)

• •

1. Preheat oven to 400°F. Spray 8-inch square baking pan with nonstick cooking spray.

2. Whisk flour, cornmeal, sugar, baking powder and salt in large bowl. Whisk milk, butter and egg in medium bowl until well blended. Add to flour mixture; stir just until dry ingredients are moistened. Pour batter into prepared pan.

3. Bake 25 minutes or until golden brown and toothpick inserted into center comes out clean. Prepare Honey Butter, if desired. Serve with corn bread.

Honey Butter

Beat 6 tablespoons (¾ stick) softened butter and
¼ cup honey in medium bowl with electric mixer at
medium-high speed until light and creamy.

COOKIES & DESSERTS

FRUITCAKE COOKIES
Makes about 6 dozen cookies

3 cups all-purpose flour

2 teaspoons baking powder

1 teaspoon baking soda

1 teaspoon salt

1 cup sugar

¾ cup shortening or softened butter

3 eggs

⅓ cup orange juice

1 tablespoon rum extract

2 cups (8 ounces) chopped candied mixed fruit

1 cup nuts, coarsely chopped

1 cup raisins

• •

1. Preheat oven to 375°F. Lightly grease cookie sheets or line with parchment paper. Whisk flour, baking powder, baking soda and salt in medium bowl.

2. Beat sugar and shortening in large bowl with electric mixer at medium speed until fluffy. Add eggs, orange juice and rum extract; beat 2 minutes. Gradually beat in flour mixture at low speed. Stir in candied fruit, nuts and raisins. Drop dough by rounded teaspoonfuls 2 inches apart onto prepared cookie sheets.

3. Bake 10 to 12 minutes or until golden brown. Cool on cookie sheets 2 minutes. Remove to wire racks; cool completely.

——— *Cookie Decorating Party* ———

Frosted Butter Cookies, page 150

Cocoa Crinkle Sandwiches, page 146

Candy Cane Biscotti, page 148

Spiced Hot Cocoa, page 176

Warm Spiced Wine, page 184

COCOA CRINKLE SANDWICHES
Makes about 20 sandwich cookies

COOKIES

1¾ cups all-purpose flour

½ cup unsweetened cocoa powder

1 teaspoon baking soda

½ teaspoon salt

½ cup (1 stick) butter

1½ cups granulated sugar, divided

2 eggs

2 teaspoons vanilla

FROSTING

2½ cups powdered sugar

1 cup (2 sticks) butter, softened

2 tablespoons unsweetened cocoa powder

½ cup dark or bittersweet chocolate chips, melted and cooled to room temperature

3 tablespoons whipping cream

1 teaspoon vanilla

⅛ teaspoon salt

• •

1. Whisk flour, ½ cup cocoa, baking soda and ½ teaspoon salt in medium bowl.

2. Melt ½ cup butter in large saucepan over medium heat; cool slightly. Add 1¼ cups granulated sugar; whisk until smooth. Add eggs, one at a time, whisking until blended after each addition. Stir in 2 teaspoons vanilla until smooth. Stir in flour mixture just until blended. Cover bowl with plastic wrap; refrigerate 2 hours.

3. Preheat oven to 350°F. Line cookie sheets with parchment paper. Shape dough into 1-inch balls. Place remaining ¼ cup granulated sugar in shallow bowl; roll balls in sugar. Place 1½ inches apart on prepared cookie sheets.

4. Bake 12 minutes or until set. Cool on cookie sheets 5 minutes. Remove to wire racks; cool completely.

5. For frosting, beat powdered sugar, 1 cup butter and 2 tablespoons cocoa in large bowl with electric mixer at medium-low speed until blended. Add chocolate, cream, 1 teaspoon vanilla and ⅛ teaspoon salt; beat until blended. Increase speed to medium-high; beat 5 minutes or until frosting is very fluffy.

6. Pipe or spread about 2 tablespoons frosting on flat sides of half of cookies; top with remaining cookies. Store leftovers in refrigerator.

CANDY CANE BISCOTTI
Makes 40 cookies

1 cup sugar

½ cup (1 stick) butter, softened

2 eggs

2 tablespoons water

1 teaspoon peppermint extract

3½ cups all-purpose flour

1 cup finely crushed peppermint candy canes, divided

½ cup slivered almonds, toasted*

1 teaspoon baking powder

½ teaspoon salt

4 ounces white chocolate, chopped, melted

To toast almonds, spread in single layer on cookie sheet. Bake in preheated 350°F oven 8 to 10 minutes or until golden brown, stirring frequently.

1. Preheat oven to 350°F. Line two cookie sheets with parchment paper.

2. Beat sugar, butter, eggs, water and peppermint extract in large bowl with electric mixer at medium speed until well blended. Add flour, ½ cup crushed candy canes, almonds, baking powder and salt. Beat at low speed just until blended.

3. Divide dough in half. Shape each half into 10×3-inch log; place each log on separate prepared cookie sheet. Bake 30 minutes or until center is firm to the touch. Let cool 15 to 20 minutes.

4. Cut logs diagonally into ½-inch slices using serrated knife; place cut sides down on prepared cookie sheets; bake 15 minutes. Turn slices over; bake 12 to 15 minutes or until edges are browned. Remove to wire racks; cool completely.

5. Dip each cookie in melted white chocolate, then in remaining ½ cup crushed candy canes.

FROSTED BUTTER COOKIES
Makes about 3 dozen cookies

3 cups all-purpose flour

1 teaspoon baking powder

½ teaspoon salt

1½ cups (3 sticks) butter, softened

¾ cup granulated sugar

3 egg yolks

2 tablespoons orange juice

1 teaspoon vanilla

Buttercream Icing or Meringue Powder Royal Icing (recipes follow)

• •

1. Whisk flour, baking powder and salt in medium bowl. Beat 1½ cups butter and granulated sugar in large bowl with electric mixer at medium-high speed until creamy. Add egg yolks, orange juice and vanilla; beat until blended. Gradually add flour mixture at low speed, beating just until blended. Shape dough into two discs; wrap in plastic wrap. Refrigerate 2 to 3 hours or until firm.

2. Preheat oven to 350°F. Roll out dough, half at a time, to ¼-inch thickness on well-floured surface. Cut dough with cookie cutters. Place 1 inch apart on ungreased cookie sheets. Bake 6 to 10 minutes or until edges are golden brown. Remove to wire racks; cool completely.

3. Prepare desired icing; tint desired colors. Place each color into piping bag filled with desired tips. Decorate cookies.

Buttercream Icing

Beat 4 cups powdered sugar, 1 cup (2 sticks) softened butter, 3 tablespoons milk, 2 teaspoons vanilla and pinch of salt in large bowl with electric mixer at low speed until blended. Beat at medium-high speed until light and fluffy.

Meringue Powder Royal Icing

Beat 6 tablespoons water and ¼ cup meringue powder in large bowl with electric mixer at low speed until well blended. Gradually beat in 1 pound powdered sugar. Increase speed to medium; beat until icing is thick and smooth. Add additional water by tablespoonfuls until icing is desired consistency. Use thicker icing to pipe details and thinner icing to fill in large areas.

CINNAMON PLUM WALNUT COBBLER
Makes 9 servings

¾ cup all-purpose flour

½ cup chopped walnuts

½ cup plus 3 tablespoons granulated sugar, divided

⅛ teaspoon salt

6 tablespoons cold butter, cut into small pieces

1 to 2 tablespoons milk, plus additional for brushing top of dough

8 red plums (about 2½ pounds), cut into ¼-inch slices

2½ tablespoons cornstarch

¾ teaspoon ground cinnamon, divided

½ cup mascarpone

2 tablespoons powdered sugar

2 tablespoons half-and-half

• •

1. Preheat oven to 350°F. Spray 8-inch square baking dish with nonstick cooking spray.

2. Combine flour, walnuts, 1 tablespoon granulated sugar and salt in food processor. Add butter; process until butter is incorporated into mixture. With motor running, add just enough milk through feed tube to form soft dough. Wrap with plastic wrap; refrigerate 30 minutes.

3. Combine plums, ½ cup granulated sugar, cornstarch and ½ teaspoon cinnamon in large bowl; toss to coat. Spread fruit mixture evenly in prepared baking dish.

4. Bake 30 minutes. Meanwhile, roll out dough into 8-inch square. Cut out nine circles with 2¼-inch round cookie cutter. Remove scraps of dough; crumble over baked fruit or discard. Arrange dough circles over fruit; brush lightly with additional milk. Combine remaining 2 tablespoons sugar and ¼ teaspoon cinnamon in small bowl; sprinkle over dough.

5. Bake 30 to 35 minutes or until topping is golden brown. Meanwhile, whisk mascarpone, powdered sugar and half-and-half in medium bowl until well blended. Serve with warm cobbler.

CARROT CAKE
Makes 8 to 10 servings

CAKE

- 2 cups all-purpose flour
- 2 teaspoons baking soda
- 2 teaspoons ground cinnamon
- 1 teaspoon salt
- 4 eggs
- 2¼ cups granulated sugar
- 1 cup vegetable oil
- 1 cup buttermilk
- 1 tablespoon vanilla
- 3 cups shredded carrots
- 3 cups walnuts, chopped and toasted,* divided
- 1 cup shredded coconut
- 1 can (8 ounces) crushed pineapple

FROSTING

- 2 packages (8 ounces each) cream cheese, softened
- 1 cup (2 sticks) butter, softened
- Pinch salt
- 3 cups powdered sugar
- 1 tablespoon orange juice
- 2 teaspoons grated orange peel
- 1 teaspoon vanilla

To toast walnuts, spread on ungreased baking sheet. Bake in preheated 350°F oven 6 to 8 minutes or until lightly browned, stirring frequently.

• •

1. Preheat oven to 350°F. Grease and flour two 9-inch round cake pans. Line bottoms of pans with parchment paper; spray paper with cooking spray.

2. For cake, whisk flour, baking soda, cinnamon and 1 teaspoon salt in medium bowl. Whisk eggs in large bowl until blended. Add granulated sugar, oil, buttermilk and 1 tablespoon vanilla; whisk until well blended. Add flour mixture; stir until well blended. Add carrots, 1 cup walnuts, coconut and pineapple; stir just until blended. Pour batter into prepared pans.

3. Bake 25 to 30 minutes or until toothpick inserted into centers comes out clean. Cool in pans 10 minutes. Remove to wire racks; cool completely.

4. For frosting, beat cream cheese, butter and pinch of salt in large bowl with electric mixer at medium speed 3 minutes or until creamy. Add powdered sugar, orange juice, orange peel and 1 teaspoon vanilla; beat at low speed until blended. Beat at medium speed 2 minutes or until frosting is smooth.

5. Place one cake layer on serving plate; spread with 2 cups frosting. Top with second cake layer; frost top and side of cake with remaining frosting. Press 1¾ cups walnuts onto side of cake. Sprinkle remaining ¼ cup walnuts over top of cake.

CHOCOLATE CARAMEL THUMBPRINT COOKIES
Makes 2½ dozen cookies

COOKIES

1½ cups all-purpose flour

¾ cup unsweetened cocoa powder

½ teaspoon salt

1 cup (2 sticks) butter, softened

⅔ cup packed brown sugar

2 eggs, separated

1 teaspoon vanilla

2 cups finely chopped pecans

CARAMEL FILLING

½ cup packed brown sugar

¼ cup (½ stick) butter

2 tablespoons whipping cream

Pinch of salt

2 tablespoons powdered sugar

• •

1. Preheat oven to 375°F. Line cookie sheets with parchment paper or leave ungreased. Whisk flour, cocoa and ½ teaspoon salt in small bowl.

2. Beat butter and ⅔ cup brown sugar in large bowl with electric mixer at medium speed until light and fluffy. Beat in egg yolks and vanilla until well blended. Gradually beat in flour mixture at low speed just until blended. Shape level tablespoonfuls of dough into balls.

3. Whisk egg whites in small bowl. Place pecans in medium bowl. Dip balls one at a time into egg whites, turning to coat completely and letting excess drip back into bowl. Roll in pecans to coat. Place on prepared cookie sheets. Press thumb firmly into center of each cookie.

4. Bake about 10 minutes until cookies are set. Quickly repress thumbprints with end of wooden spoon. Cool on cookie sheets 5 minutes. Remove to wire rack; cool completely.

5. For filling, combine ½ cup brown sugar and ¼ cup butter in small saucepan. Cook over medium heat until mixture begins to boil, stirring constantly; boil 1 minute, stirring constantly. Remove from heat. Stir in cream and pinch of salt; cool 15 minutes. Whisk in powdered sugar until smooth. Fill each cookie with about ½ teaspoon filling; let stand until firm.

CINNAMON GINGER PUMPKIN PIE
Makes 8 servings

1 refrigerated pie crust (half of 14-ounce package)

1 tablespoon sugar

1 tablespoon ground cinnamon

2 teaspoons ground ginger

1 teaspoon ground cloves

1 teaspoon ground nutmeg

½ teaspoon salt

3 eggs

2½ teaspoons vanilla

1 can (15 ounces) pumpkin

⅓ cup sour cream

1 can (14 ounces) sweetened condensed milk

Whole pecans (optional)

Sweetened whipped cream (optional)

• •

1. Preheat oven to 425°F. Fit pie crust into 9-inch deep dish pie plate; flute edge.

2. Combine sugar, cinnamon, ginger, cloves, nutmeg and salt in large bowl; mix well. Whisk in eggs and vanilla until smooth. Add pumpkin and sour cream; whisk until smooth. Gradually stir in sweetened condensed milk; mix until well blended. Pour into crust.

3. Bake 15 minutes. *Reduce oven temperature to 350°F.* Bake 40 to 45 minutes or until knife inserted near center comes out clean. Cool on wire rack at least 1½ hours before cutting. Garnish with pecans and whipped cream.

TRIPLE GINGER COOKIES
Makes 3 dozen cookies

2 cups all-purpose flour

2 teaspoons baking soda

1 teaspoon ground ginger

½ teaspoon salt

¾ cup (1½ sticks) butter

1¼ cups sugar, divided

¼ cup molasses

1 egg

1 tablespoon finely minced fresh ginger

1 tablespoon finely minced crystallized ginger*

*Look for softer, larger slices of ginger at natural foods or specialty stores. If using the small dry cubes of ginger, steep the cubes in boiling hot water a few minutes to soften, then drain, pat dry and mince.

1. Whisk flour, baking soda, ground ginger and salt in medium bowl.

2. Melt butter in small heavy saucepan over low heat; pour into large bowl and cool slightly. Add 1 cup sugar, molasses and egg; beat with electric mixer at medium speed until well blended. Gradually beat in flour mixture at low speed just until blended. Add fresh ginger and crystallized ginger; mix just until blended. Cover; refrigerate 1 hour.

3. Preheat oven to 375°F. Line cookie sheets with parchment paper or lightly grease. Place remaining ¼ cup sugar in small bowl. Roll dough into 1-inch balls. Add to sugar; roll to coat. Place 3 inches apart on prepared cookie sheets. (If dough is very sticky, drop by teaspoonfuls into sugar to coat.)

4. For chewy cookies, bake 7 minutes or until edges just start to brown. For crisper cookies, bake 2 to 4 minutes longer. Cool on cookie sheets 1 minute. Remove to wire racks; cool completely.

Variation

Roll dough in plastic food wrap to form a log. Refrigerate up to one week or freeze up to two months until needed. Bring the dough nearly to room temperature and slice. Dip the tops in sugar and bake as instructed.

LITTLE CHRISTMAS TRUFFLES

Makes about 3½ dozen treats

1 can (14 ounces) sweetened
   condensed milk

1 ounce semisweet chocolate

2 teaspoons vanilla

2¼ cups chocolate sandwich
   cookie crumbs

⅓ cup white chocolate chips

Green sprinkles

Small red candies

• •

1. Combine sweetened condensed milk and semisweet chocolate in medium saucepan; cook and stir over low heat until chocolate is melted and mixture is smooth. Pour into medium bowl; stir in vanilla.

2. Stir cookie crumbs into chocolate mixture until well blended. Cover and refrigerate 1 hour.

3. Line baking sheet with waxed paper. Shape heaping teaspoonfuls of chocolate mixture into 1-inch balls. Place on prepared baking sheet. Refrigerate until firm.

4. Place balls in 1¾-inch paper or foil baking cups on baking sheets. Place white chocolate chips in small microwavable bowl. Microwave on MEDIUM (50%) 1 minute or until melted, stirring after 30 seconds. Spoon melted white chocolate over tops of balls. Top with sprinkles and red candies. Let stand until set. Store covered in refrigerator.

APPLE-PEAR PRALINE PIE
Makes 8 servings

Double-Crust Pie Pastry (recipe follows)

4 cups sliced peeled Granny Smith apples

2 cups sliced peeled pears

¾ cup granulated sugar

¼ cup plus 1 tablespoon all-purpose flour, divided

4 teaspoons ground cinnamon

¼ teaspoon salt

½ cup (1 stick) plus 2 tablespoons butter, divided

1 cup packed brown sugar

1 tablespoon half-and-half or milk

1 cup chopped pecans

• •

1. Prepare Double-Crust Pie Pastry.

2. Combine apples, pears, granulated sugar, ¼ cup flour, cinnamon and salt in large bowl; toss to coat. Let stand 15 minutes.

3. Preheat oven to 350°F. Roll out one disc of pastry into 11-inch circle on floured surface. Line deep-dish 9-inch pie plate with pastry; sprinkle with remaining 1 tablespoon flour. Spoon apple and pear mixture into crust; dot with 2 tablespoons butter. Roll out remaining disc of pastry into 10-inch circle. Place over fruit; seal and flute edge. Cut slits in top crust.

4. Bake 1 hour. Meanwhile, combine remaining ½ cup butter, brown sugar and half-and-half in small saucepan; bring to a boil over medium heat, stirring frequently. Boil 2 minutes, stirring constantly. Remove from heat; stir in pecans. Spread over pie.

5. Cool pie on wire rack 15 minutes. Serve warm or at room temperature.

Double-Crust Pie Pastry

Combine 2½ cups all-purpose flour, 1 teaspoon granulated sugar and 1 teaspoon salt in large bowl. Cut in 1 cup (2 sticks) cold cubed butter with pastry blender or two knives until coarse crumbs form. Drizzle ⅓ cup ice water over flour mixture, 2 tablespoons at a time, stirring just until dough comes together. Divide dough in half. Shape each half into disc; wrap in plastic wrap. Refrigerate 30 minutes.

FRENCH SILK PIE
Makes 8 servings

1 (9-inch) deep-dish pie crust (frozen or refrigerated)

1⅓ cups granulated sugar

¾ cup (1½ sticks) butter, softened

4 ounces unsweetened chocolate, melted

1½ tablespoons unsweetened cocoa powder

1 teaspoon vanilla

⅛ teaspoon salt

4 pasteurized eggs*

1 cup whipping cream

2 tablespoons powdered sugar

Chocolate curls (optional)

The eggs in this recipe are not cooked, so use pasteurized eggs to ensure food safety.

• •

1. Bake pie crust according to package directions. Cool completely on wire rack.

2. Beat granulated sugar and butter in large bowl with electric mixer at medium speed 4 minutes or until light and fluffy. Add melted chocolate, cocoa, vanilla and salt; beat until well blended. Add eggs, one at a time, beating 4 minutes after each addition and scraping down side of bowl occasionally.

3. Spread filling in cooled crust. Refrigerate at least 3 hours or overnight.

4. Beat cream and powdered sugar in medium bowl with electric mixer at high speed until soft peaks form. Pipe or spread whipped cream over chocolate layer; garnish with chocolate curls.

CHOCOLATE-PUMPKIN CAKE WITH COCONUT PECAN FROSTING

Makes 12 servings

2 cups all-purpose flour

⅔ cup unsweetened cocoa powder

1 cup quick-cooking oats

1 tablespoon ground cinnamon

2 teaspoons baking powder

1 teaspoon baking soda

1 teaspoon salt

½ teaspoon ground cloves

2 cups granulated sugar

1½ cups (3 sticks) butter, softened, divided

4 eggs

1 can (15 ounces) pumpkin

1 can (8 ounces) crushed pineapple

1 teaspoon almond extract

1 cup packed brown sugar

½ cup whole milk or half-and-half

1½ cups flaked coconut

1½ cups pecans, chopped

. . . .

1. Preheat oven to 350°F. Grease and flour 13×9-inch baking pan. Whisk flour, cocoa, oats, cinnamon, baking powder, baking soda, salt and cloves in medium bowl.

2. Beat granulated sugar and 1 cup butter in large bowl with electric mixer at medium-high speed 3 minutes or until creamy. Add eggs, one at a time, beating well after each addition. Add pumpkin, pineapple and almond extract; beat until well blended. Gradually beat in flour mixture at low speed just until blended. Spread batter in prepared pan.

3. Bake 40 to 45 minutes or until toothpick inserted into center comes out clean.

4. Preheat broiler. Melt remaining ½ cup butter in medium saucepan over low heat. Stir in brown sugar and milk until smooth. Stir in coconut and pecans. Spread frosting over warm cake.

5. Broil 3 to 4 inches from heat source 3 to 4 minutes or until frosting is golden brown and bubbling. Cool completely in pan on wire rack.

CHOCOLATE CITRUS TRIANGLES
Makes about 2 dozen

24 chocolate sandwich cookies

1 cup (2 sticks) plus 6 tablespoons butter, softened, divided

3 cups powdered sugar, plus additional for dusting

2 tablespoons whipping cream or milk

1 tablespoon grated orange peel

1 teaspoon grated lemon peel

½ teaspoon vanilla

• •

1. Line 9-inch square baking pan with parchment paper. Place cookies and 10 tablespoons butter in food processor or blender; process to fine crumbs. Press onto bottom of prepared pan. Refrigerate 1 hour or until firm.

2. Combine 3 cups powdered sugar, remaining 12 tablespoons butter, cream, orange peel, lemon peel and vanilla in large bowl. Beat with electric mixer at medium speed 3 to 5 minutes or until blended. Spread over crust.

3. Refrigerate 2 hours or until firm. Cut into 1-inch squares; cut in half to form triangles. Sprinkle with additional powdered sugar just before serving. Store leftovers in refrigerator.

LEMON ICED AMBROSIA BARS

Makes 2 to 3 dozen bars

1¾ cups all-purpose flour, divided

2⅓ cups powdered sugar, divided

½ teaspoon salt, divided

¾ cup (1½ sticks) cold butter

2 cups packed brown sugar

4 eggs, beaten

1 cup flaked coconut

1 cup finely chopped pecans

½ teaspoon baking powder

2 cups powdered sugar

3 tablespoons lemon juice

2 tablespoons butter, softened

1. Preheat oven to 350°F. Grease 13×9-inch baking pan.

2. Combine 1½ cups flour, ⅓ cup powdered sugar and ¼ teaspoon salt in medium bowl; cut in butter with pastry blender or fingertips until mixture resembles coarse crumbs. Press onto bottom of prepared pan; bake 15 minutes.

3. Meanwhile, combine remaining ¼ cup flour, brown sugar, eggs, coconut, pecans, baking powder and remaining ¼ teaspoon salt in medium bowl; mix well. Spread evenly over baked crust; bake 20 minutes. Cool completely in pan on wire rack.

4. For icing, stir together powdered sugar, lemon juice and softened butter until smooth. Spread over bars. Cover and refrigerate until glaze is set. Cut into rectangles. Store, covered, in refrigerator.

DRINKS & PUNCHES

SPICED HOT COCOA →
Makes 8 servings

⅔ cup water
1 cup sugar
½ cup unsweetened cocoa powder
1 tablespoon all-purpose flour
2 teaspoons ground cinnamon
1½ teaspoons ground cloves

½ teaspoon salt
½ teaspoon chili powder
¼ teaspoon ground allspice
8 cups milk
1½ teaspoons vanilla
Mini marshmallows

• •

1. Bring water to a boil in medium saucepan over high heat. Whisk sugar, cocoa powder, flour, cinnamon, cloves, salt, chili powder and allspice into saucepan, stirring constantly. Reduce heat to medium; cook and stir 1 to 2 minutes or until thick and smooth.

2. Stir in milk and vanilla. Cook until hot, stirring frequently. Pour into mugs and top with marshmallows.

KIR
Makes 1 serving

½ ounce crème de cassis (black currant liqueur)

¾ cup chilled dry white wine

• •

Pour crème de cassis into white wine glass; pour in white wine.

Kir Royale
Replace white wine with chilled champagne or sparkling wine; serve in champagne flute.

STRAWBERRY CHAMPAGNE PUNCH →
Makes 12 servings

2 packages (10 ounces each) frozen sliced strawberries in syrup, thawed

2 cans (5½ ounces each) apricot or peach nectar

¼ cup lemon juice

2 tablespoons honey

2 bottles (750 ml each) champagne or sparkling white wine, chilled

. . . .

1. Place strawberries with syrup in food processor or blender; process until smooth.

2. Pour puréed strawberries into large punch bowl. Stir in apricot nectar, lemon juice and honey; blend well. Refrigerate until ready to serve.

3. Just before serving, stir champagne into strawberry mixture.

GROG
Makes 1 serving

2 ounces dark rum

½ ounce lemon juice

1 teaspoon packed brown sugar

2 to 3 whole cloves

¾ cup boiling water

1 cinnamon stick

. . . .

Combine rum, lemon juice, brown sugar and cloves in warm mug. Pour in boiling water; stir with cinnamon stick until brown sugar is dissolved.

TRIPLE DELICIOUS HOT CHOCOLATE
Makes 6 servings

3 cups milk, divided

⅓ cup sugar

¼ cup unsweetened cocoa powder

¼ teaspoon salt

¾ teaspoon vanilla

1 cup whipping cream

1 ounce white chocolate, chopped

1 ounce bittersweet chocolate, chopped

Whipped cream

Mini chocolate chips or shaved bittersweet chocolate

• •

Slow Cooker Directions

1. Combine ½ cup milk, sugar, cocoa and salt in medium bowl; whisk until smooth. Pour into slow cooker. Add remaining 2½ cups milk and vanilla. Cover; cook on LOW 2 hours.

2. Add cream. Cover and cook on LOW 10 minutes. Stir in white and bittersweet chocolates until melted.

3. Ladle hot chocolate into mugs; top with whipped cream and chocolate chips.

EGGNOG →
Makes 1 serving

1½ ounces brandy

½ cup milk

1 pasteurized egg

2 teaspoons simple syrup*

¼ teaspoon vanilla

Freshly grated nutmeg

*To make simple syrup, combine 1 cup water and 1 cup sugar in small saucepan; cook and stir over medium heat just until sugar dissolves. Cool to room temperature; store in glass jar in refrigerator.

• •

Fill cocktail shaker half full with ice; add brandy, milk, egg, syrup and vanilla. Shake until blended; strain into mug or glass. Sprinkle with nutmeg.

Blender Variation

Blend brandy, milk, egg, syrup and vanilla in blender; pour into glass. Sprinkle with nutmeg.

POMEGRANATE MIMOSA
Makes 8 servings

2 cups chilled pomegranate juice

1 bottle (750 ml) chilled champagne

Pomegranate seeds

• •

Pour pomegranate juice into eight champagne flutes; top with champagne. Garnish with pomegranate seeds.

SPARKLING POMEGRANATE GINGERADE →
Makes 4 servings

½ cup sugar

¼ cup water

1 teaspoon grated lemon peel

1 (1-inch) piece fresh ginger, thinly sliced

2 cups seltzer water or sparkling wine

2 cups pomegranate juice

Ice

. . . .

1. Combine sugar, water, lemon peel and ginger in small saucepan. Bring mixture to a boil over medium heat. Boil 1 minute. Remove from heat; cool completely.

2. Strain syrup into large pitcher. Stir in seltzer water and pomegranate juice. Serve over ice.

WARM SPICED WINE
Makes ½ gallon

8 cups dry red wine (about 2½ bottles)

2 oranges, peeled and sliced

3 tablespoons packed brown sugar or honey

6 cardamom pods

3 cinnamon sticks

3 whole star anise

3 whole cloves

½ cup brandy (optional)

. . . .

1. Combine wine, oranges, brown sugar, cardamom pods, cinnamon sticks, star anise and cloves in large saucepan. Heat over medium-low heat 20 minutes or until warm. (Do not boil or allow temperature to exceed 165°F).

2. Remove and discard orange slices and spices before serving. Stir in brandy, if desired.

HOT MULLED CIDER →
Makes 16 servings

8 cups (½ gallon) apple cider

½ cup packed brown sugar

1½ teaspoons balsamic or cider vinegar

1 teaspoon vanilla

1 cinnamon stick

6 whole cloves

½ cup applejack or bourbon (optional)

. . . .

Combine apple cider, brown sugar, vinegar, vanilla, cinnamon stick and cloves in large saucepan; bring to a boil over medium-high heat. Reduce heat to low; simmer 30 minutes. Remove and discard cinnamon stick and cloves. Stir in applejack, if desired. Serve warm.

MOCHA NOG
Makes 8 servings

1 quart eggnog

2 tablespoons unsweetened cocoa powder

1 tablespoon instant coffee granules

¼ cup coffee-flavored liqueur

Whipped cream (optional)

. . . .

1. Heat eggnog, cocoa and coffee granules in large saucepan over medium heat until mixture is heated through and coffee granules are dissolved, whisking frequently; do not boil. Remove from heat; stir in coffee liqueur.

2. Pour eggnog into individual mugs. Top with whipped cream, if desired.

INDEX

188

METRIC CONVERSION CHART

VOLUME MEASUREMENTS (dry)

$^1/_8$ teaspoon = 0.5 mL
$^1/_4$ teaspoon = 1 mL
$^1/_2$ teaspoon = 2 mL
$^3/_4$ teaspoon = 4 mL
1 teaspoon = 5 mL
1 tablespoon = 15 mL
2 tablespoons = 30 mL
$^1/_4$ cup = 60 mL
$^1/_3$ cup = 75 mL
$^1/_2$ cup = 125 mL
$^2/_3$ cup = 150 mL
$^3/_4$ cup = 175 mL
1 cup = 250 mL
2 cups = 1 pint = 500 mL
3 cups = 750 mL
4 cups = 1 quart = 1 L

VOLUME MEASUREMENTS (fluid)

1 fluid ounce (2 tablespoons) = 30 mL
4 fluid ounces ($^1/_2$ cup) = 125 mL
8 fluid ounces (1 cup) = 250 mL
12 fluid ounces (1$^1/_2$ cups) = 375 mL
16 fluid ounces (2 cups) = 500 mL

WEIGHTS (mass)

$^1/_2$ ounce = 15 g
1 ounce = 30 g
3 ounces = 90 g
4 ounces = 120 g
8 ounces = 225 g
10 ounces = 285 g
12 ounces = 360 g
16 ounces = 1 pound = 450 g

DIMENSIONS

$^1/_{16}$ inch = 2 mm
$^1/_8$ inch = 3 mm
$^1/_4$ inch = 6 mm
$^1/_2$ inch = 1.5 cm
$^3/_4$ inch = 2 cm
1 inch = 2.5 cm

OVEN TEMPERATURES

250°F = 120°C
275°F = 140°C
300°F = 150°C
325°F = 160°C
350°F = 180°C
375°F = 190°C
400°F = 200°C
425°F = 220°C
450°F = 230°C

BAKING PAN SIZES

Utensil	Size in Inches/Quarts	Metric Volume	Size in Centimeters
Baking or Cake Pan (square or rectangular)	8×8×2	2 L	20×20×5
	9×9×2	2.5 L	23×23×5
	12×8×2	3 L	30×20×5
	13×9×2	3.5 L	33×23×5
Loaf Pan	8×4×3	1.5 L	20×10×7
	9×5×3	2 L	23×13×7
Round Layer Cake Pan	8×1½	1.2 L	20×4
	9×1½	1.5 L	23×4
Pie Plate	8×1¼	750 mL	20×3
	9×1¼	1 L	23×3
Baking Dish or Casserole	1 quart	1 L	—
	1½ quart	1.5 L	—
	2 quart	2 L	—